THE THINGS THEY WROTE

Sarah A. · Elizabeth Armstrong · Sarah Baron

Sandra Beirne · Deborah Bernstein · Diane Birnbaumer

Annie Bustin · Jennifer Caputo-Seidler

Karen Dybner-Madero · Brittany Ebey · Sarah Edwards

Rachel Kadar · Caroline Kechejian · Margaret Lamkin

Owen Lee-Park · Barbara Lovenheim · Kerry L. Malawista

Danielle H. Maxonight · Elizabeth Mitchell

Denise Montagnino · Candida Moreira · Gavin Morrison

Debra A. Neumann · Susan Perron · Shobana Ramasamy

Blaine Robinson · Dipanwita Saha · Tarah Salazar

Janna Sandmeyer · Amelia Sauter · Michael Schmitz

Adrienne Smith · Craig R. Sussman · Margaret Tehven

Debra Thompson · Melissa Vargas · Joanne Wilkinson

Savannah J. Willingham · Anna Wright

The Things They Wrote:
A writing/healing project

EDITED BY

Kerry L. Malawista, Ph.D.

Published in the United States by **ROOM: A Sketchbook for Analytic *Action***

ISBN: 978-1-960680-00-6

BOOK DESIGNED BY BOYD DELANCEY

This book is dedicated to all the frontline healthcare workers who, day after day, put their lives on the line to help others.

CONTENTS

ACKNOWLEDGMENTS

I am forever grateful to the remarkable volunteers who selflessly gave their time, compassion, and support; without their dedication TTC could never have succeeded. Special thanks to Elissa Ely and Ruth Neubauer for the extraordinary number of workshops they led and their continual help moving the project into new arenas.

Sara Taber for having the expertise and empathy to create such a powerful training for our volunteers.

My enormous debt of gratitude to Hattie Myers for creating **ROOM: A Sketchbook for Analytic *Action*** and her enthusiastic lead in getting this project out in the world. My thanks to Claire Oleson and Aiyana White for their many hours of work during the first phase of this project. Additionally, I am thankful to Boyd Delancey for his final editing of this manuscript.

My appreciation to Tim O'Brien, whose novel *The Things They Carried* this project is named for. And my husband, Alan Heilbron, who without his constant source of support and inspiration the project would never have launched.

INTRODUCTION

A Passage Out of Pandemic Loss: Grief and Trauma into the Faraway Nearby

Kerry L. Malawista, Ph.D.

SIX STRANGERS STARED AT ME THROUGH THE SCREEN ON the day of our first writing workshop. "The Things They Carry Project," an initiative aimed at helping health care workers and first responders find their way through grief, was off and running. Across the country, some two dozen workshops gathered on the internet. In each, a therapist and writer would lead medical caretakers through writing prompts that invited them to tell their stories. Here was the place they could let down their guard, perhaps lighten their load.

In all the groups I've run these past months, these stories linger in my mind.

This time, an ER doctor spoke first. "All year I saw COVID-19 deaths.

Most days I lost count," he said. "I didn't want to tell my family the horrors I saw, so I tried to hide how wrecked I felt. Now that things are calmer—getting back to normal—I don't know how to find my way back to them." He turned his head so we wouldn't see his tears.

The Zoom yellow border surrounding another participant's box lit up. A nurse's aide said, "I can't get a conversation out of my head, and it replays over and over—driving me crazy." She took a deep breath and continued in her southern drawl, "A patient's husband was holdin' the phone to her ear. I don't think she was even conscious, but I heard her daughter weeping, tellin' her mama goodbye, that she loves her." Now the aide was crying too.

Until now, in the face of exhaustion, terror, and hopelessness, these people simply carried on, with no time to think about all that they were experiencing. What are they to do now?

I understand loss. In 30-plus years as a psychotherapist, I have heard stories of trauma, despair, and pain. Witnessing a horror or experiencing a trauma can silence us, leaving us unmoored, alienated from those we need and love most. But giving words to the unspeakable, to all we have lost, is necessary. We need to say: *this is what happened to me*— somewhere, and to someone.

Nobody can undo the pain and sorrow these health care workers and many of the rest of us have experienced this past year. Writing about the experience may be one way through it. Writing enables us to step back and reflect on the "before and after" of trauma and loss. Creating a narrative of what happened can also be healing, as we find the words to replace our silent trauma. I've come to understand that writing can transform fear, dread, and pain from inchoate and disjointed images into reimagined memories that one can begin to bear.

This understanding, though, did not just come from listening to my patients. When I lost my 18-year-old daughter, Sarah, I was left adrift, pummeled by grief. Curiously, it was Sarah who helped me through by teaching me, years before I would fully grasp the meaning, about the middle distance.

It was a year after Sarah died. My husband and I were attending a Georgia O'Keeffe show at the Phillips Museum in Washington, DC. Roaming the galleries, I was taken with O'Keeffe's flowers of red, yellow, and purple, each appearing as if under a microscope. One painting stopped me in my tracks.

I couldn't take my eyes off it as I tried to understand the unsettled, off-kilter feeling it created in me.

The canvas showed the remains of a massive elk's skull and antlers suspended over a range of light-filled crimson mountains, rising up from the desert sand. I was struck by the juxtaposition: a bright, radiant light, and this looming marker of death. The title was printed in black letters on a white card at the lower left of the frame: "From the Faraway, Nearby."

Suddenly I was back in Sarah's bedroom; she was 15 at the time, already a painter, and telling me about something she called the middle distance. To demonstrate, she pulled an art book off her bedroom shelf and flipped to a painting by Jean François Millet called "The Gleaners." She pointed to a figure on the right, a woman bending over to collect the last bits of wheat after the harvest. By foreshortening the space between the distant haystacks and the nearby wheat gatherers, Millet had created the illusion that the figures were larger than life, overpowering the scene.

"See, the middle distance is what gives a painting balance," Sarah told me.

Gazing at O'Keeffe's painting many years later, I could see what Sarah had meant. Without a middle distance, the elk's remains dominate the foreground, while the mountains are eerily far away. O'Keeffe had left out the bridge between them, their shared middle ground.

And suddenly I had a context for how I had felt since Sarah's death. In the foreground, Sarah was still here, unbearably yet thrillingly close, as though she might appear at any moment. I imagined catching a glimpse of her just around the corner; I would plan a vegan dinner that I knew she would like; I couldn't wait for her to get home to tell her how unhappy I had been since she died. I was in a constant state of suspended disbelief. Yet I couldn't give it up. I feared Sarah being completely lost to me—stranded off in the distance, in a mist settling over a distant mountain range.

I was in a "faraway, nearby" place. I could neither bring her back nor let her go.

O'Keeffe's painting and those three simple words, "The Faraway, Nearby," gave meaning to what I was experiencing. Finding the middle distance was essential, a space to bear the unbearable and acknowledge the unreachable.

I needed a bridge between the nearby–the immediate and unending pain of losing Sarah–and the faraway desolate horizon of life without her.

Never thinking myself a writer, I nonetheless began jotting down thoughts about O'Keeffe and then images and memories of Sarah. I was inscribing Sarah, and bit by bit she came to life on the page. Writing became my way of carrying her with me, of beginning to fathom how to be in a world without my daughter, of finding a language for my loss.

Our writing workshops offered this process to those who sacrificed so much during the pandemic: a space to reflect on the past year, an invitation to creatively express what they have been through, and an audience to receive their stories. I hoped that offering these workshops would give a chance for them to discover a newfound resilience and creativity, not in the sense of making great art, but in finding a potential that exists in all of us, to express ourselves in our own unique way.

As I scan each set of new faces in our Zoom sessions, I imagine the participants feeling relieved, perhaps recognizing that moving forward rests on an understanding of where they have been. The act of filling a blank page itself pushes us into the future. By writing their experiences, as I did mine, they can make their way toward the middle distance.

☀ ☀ ☀

How "The Things They Carry Project" Began

In March 2020, one year after the devastating COVID-19 pandemic shut down our nation, my therapy practice was overflowing with stressed and grief-stricken patients. Among them were two frontline health care workers struggling with the exhaustion from the double-shifts they were pulling, the countless deaths that continued to haunt them.

As one ICU doctor spoke of the horror of being unable to intubate a twenty-eight-year-old woman and watching her die. I thought of the words of Tim O'Brien, the author of *The Things They Carried:* "I carry the memories of the ghosts of a place called Vietnam."

Frontline health care workers, having witnessed death on a massive scale during the pandemic, report the same symptoms as soldiers returning from war: anxiety, panic attacks, depression, irritability, and exhaustion. And, yet, in the face of all this sorrow and strife frontline workers had rallied. Like good soldiers, they did their duty, served in the trenches fighting Covid, with no time to think about all that they had experienced.

How would my patients and other frontline workers process the past year and a half?

I suggested to the ICU doctor that she might try writing about what she had witnessed. As a writer and co-chair of New Directions in Writing[1], I knew that, like talk therapy, writing can provide a path to processing traumatic memory, giving shape and meaning to an unprocessed experience. I understood that paradoxically one can be enlivened by writing about death.

A few weeks later, my patient told me how she found meaning and solace in the act of putting words to all that she experienced. Writing allowed her to take what was unformed in the body, that lacked a verbal narrative, and move it to a level that could be symbolized with words.

In that moment, "The Things They Carry Project" was conceived. Healthcare workers who had served their time on the frontlines might be served by writing about it. Though writing could neither change the events they had experienced nor eliminate their devastating pain and sorrow, putting words to their struggle might bring comfort. As Virginia Woolf told her biographer Nigel Nicolson, "Nothing has really happened until it has been described."

With that idea in mind, I reached out to the New Directions community of therapists and writers across the country. Within 24 hours, my email had elicited more than 120 volunteers. I had unwittingly tapped into a powerful desire and spirit to serve the community.

---

1 New Directions in Writing is a three-year training program that brings together clinicians, academicians, and writers to foster intellectual growth and enhance participants' ability to write about personal and professional topics.

In less than three weeks, we had a website, and 60-plus pairs of therapists and writers eager to donate their time leading free writing groups for first responders. After participating in a three-hour training technique called "Writing for Resilience," our volunteers were ready to go, each agreeing to run three, 90-minute Zoom workshops.

The groups offered conversation and writing prompts, allowing six participants to explore their COVID-19 experiences, share their writing, listen, and respond to each other. In addition to the writing itself, sharing stories and traumas with others in the trenches can hasten healing by breaking through the isolation that often accompanies pain.

As of January 1, 2023, more than 900 participants—from all over the United States, as well as internationally, including from Africa, Brazil, Mexico, and Pakistan have completed a workshop, with many continuing in the recently added alumni groups. These ad hoc groups bring together nurses, health aides, doctors, clergy, and hospice workers. People of different ages, races, and education levels, all sharing the turmoil of this pandemic through their writing.

The essays and poems offered here speak to the transformative power of these workshops. The Things They Carry Project created an opportunity for re-vision, a new way for participants to reflect on the past year and the possibility of imagining a more hopeful future.

Their writing lets us know what they went through—since hospitals were off-limits to visitors and reporters and the workers themselves were too compromised at the time to tell even the people in their lives what was going on. Reading these selections recognizes and honors their commitment, allowing us to witness and empathize with both their experience and its aftermath.

Yet while the frontline workers have carried the heaviest load, each one of us has borne witness and likely bear scars from the pandemic. In time we may all need to find the words, and to tell our stories, of living in the time of COVID-19.

☀ ☀ ☀

More about the Workshops: Writing for Resilience

Once the spark for the project was ignited, I turned to New Directions faculty member Sara Mansfield Taber to offer a three-hour training to the writers and therapists who had volunteered to guide the workshops. Sara, a writer and psychotherapist, had run similar writing workshops for KIND (Kids in Need of Defense) volunteers, who provided legal and other support to unaccompanied immigrant minors. These KIND volunteers, having seen the horrors at the border, were soon suffering from post-traumatic stress disorder (PTSD) and vicarious trauma. The workshops that Sara led for them tapped into Louise de Salvo's Writing as a Way of Healing, and we planned to do the same.

De Salvo says that writing allows us to sort through, reflect on, and organize what puzzles and troubles us—to discover meaning and to gain psychic freedom. According to her, "Writing permits the construction of a cohesive, elaborate, thoughtful personal narrative in the way that simply speaking about our experiences doesn't. Through writing, suffering can be transmuted into art."[2]

Our workshops are co-led by a writer and a therapist who understand that weathering trauma and finding personal growth requires one to transform the experience, gain insight, and find internal resources to keep calm and strong. The Things They Carry Project uses writing to step back and reflect on the "before and after" of trauma. Creating a narrative promotes healing; the story of what happened to us imposes order and provides insight to what might otherwise seem only like chaos or mayhem. If we can begin to make sense of all that, we can come to a new understanding that allows for emotional healing.

---

2   Desalvo, L. 2000. Writing as a Way of Healing. New York: Beacon Press. p. 41.

The workshops offer a confidential and nurturing environment where participants write, share their writing with others (this is voluntary), and listen to others' stories. Writing in the company of others has special benefits. To have other writers witness and validate one's experiences relieves isolation and creates a sense of solidarity.

This safe forum allows members to reflect on the meaning of the stories they write and hear, and to experience a sense of community. Ideally, each participant will gain a greater sense of personal peace and agency and identify the ways their professional work has enriched their lives.

During each workshop, therapist-writer pairs offered writing prompts for participants to explore two important aspects of their experience:

1. Put into words the troubling experiences they have had during the COVID-19 pandemic—to delve into the details and possible meanings of these experiences, to express their past and current feelings, and to record the insights they have gained through these challenging, distressing, and deeply moving encounters.

2. Write out self-care practices they cultivated to find balance and recover from their troubling experiences.

The initial prompt asked participants to write about their safe place, what gives them comfort in difficult times. This could be a person, place, an object, even a memory. We then asked participants to recall a time of resiliency, allowing them to locate a sense of courage and strength in the past before examining the tough aspects of the present. With each workshop, the prompts deepened, moving toward writing about the more challenging, traumatic moments. We remind them to not worry over grammar or to perfect the language. They could choose to do that later.

Following the free-writes, participants have an opportunity to share their words, to respond to and reflect on the writing they have produced or heard. Our hope is that participants come away with a deepened sense of shared humanity and camaraderie in the human struggle—and a more secure sense of personal equanimity and strength to keep them going in their vital work and service on behalf of others.

The Things They Wrote

PART I

Gearing Up

INTRODUCTION

Kerry L. Malawista, Ph.D.

FRONTLINE WORKERS SHARING THE FRIGHTENING EARLY days of COVID-19 describe isolated moments when the overwhelming dangers they faced slowly began to seep in. We witness the careful, methodical practice of nurses and physicians gearing up for all they must carry, as they change into PPE, personal protective equipment, and PAPR, powered air purifying respirators. We see them donning blue scrubs and hear the snap of gloves. Hands cracked and bleeding from constant hand washing. We smell the fear filling the N95 mask, and we imagine not only the isolation under the PAPR hood but also the terror:

At the start there were so many questions and no answers. Was the person who wore this hood before me infected? Could they infect themselves just by removing their PPE? How long can the virus live on a surface? How much time can they be around a patient and not risk getting sick? Will intubating a patient to get them on a ventilator mean sending molecules of the Covid virus airborne? The terror of getting it wrong and possibly dying.

For frontline workers, the never-ending necessity to protect themselves from patients, from colleagues, and from visitors is painful. They have spent more than a year isolated, masked, and sacrificing their health for others. Not wanting to burden or frighten family members they have remained silenced. Worse is the worry about protecting family members from them as they return home each night.

Yet, beneath all the hot and itchy layers of protective gear, all the effort to safeguard their health, their humanity endures—offering profound moments of connection. For nurse Caroline Kechejian, snapping on her gray non-latex gloves symbolizes that she is ready to face the day. Declaring herself equipped for the next challenge, the gloves are her way of saying, "I am here."

Patient prep during COVID-19 times has meant a readiness infused with dread. Physician assistant Adrienne Smith writes about a patient's wife who shared with her the comfort she finds in the Japanese art of paper folding. Like prepping to see a patient, creating an origami crane involves its own step-by-step process: the origami process is calming and restorative, each step its own meditation. Included in the practice is an ancient promise, that anyone who folds a thousand cranes will be granted eternal good fortune or healing.

Sharing this moment with the patient's wife moves Adrienne Smith to return to her patient wearing only a mask, not the previous hood. She sits with him, reading aloud the many cards he has received from family. Later that evening, she phones to check on her patient, who has returned home to hospice care. When she hears the wife's acceptance and gratitude, her stored-up pain breaks through. She "crumbles in the presence of her [the wife's] strength . . . at the human capacity to love despite the pain."

Care-giving, like origami, requires discipline and focus. So does writing. In the act and art of filling a blank white page, creativity and healing can transform pain into something beautiful.

Gloves

Caroline Kechejian, RN
Cardiac Unit • New York, NY

A pair of gray non-latex gloves, size small. I run in to a patient's room to prevent them from falling out of bed or to give them an emergency dose of a lifesaving medication and without thought, I look down at my hands. There are gloves on them. When did I put these on? I can't recall. But it feels like I'm wearing my hands now. They are smooth and elastic and they smell like rubber—but gloves rubber, not car-tire rubber. They protect me. They protect my patients. I know where my next pair sits in a box on the wall in case I need back up. I can probably put these gloves on in under 5 seconds, though I've never actually timed it. I can hear the *SNAP!* they make when I'm *really* ready to go. I am a nurse, yes. But with a pair of gray non-latex gloves, I *know* I am ready; I am here.

Origami

Adrienne Smith

Physician Assistant ● Utah

I was on the second day of a seven-day stretch on the inpatient internal medicine service. The patient had transferred out of the ICU during the night. He was a relatively healthy man who had contracted COVID-19, required intubation, and suffered two strokes during the acute phase of his illness. He was one of my earliest COVID-19 patients, and I was awkward with the donning of the PAPR and PPE. I walked onto the locked-down unit around 8 am and took off my athletic layer, stethoscope, and badge, piling them on a cart outside of his room.

I felt suddenly vulnerable in my cotton t-shirt and scrub pants, bereft of confidence or authority as I began what became a familiar ritual.

I pull on a pair of blue latex gloves and tear a pungent bleach wipe from the purple cylinder mounted on the wall. With this, I wipe down the thick black plastic belt that holds the PAPR battery pack. It clicks satisfyingly around my waist like a gunslinger belt, and I struggle to cinch it to my waistline. It whirrs to life like a metallic insect. I methodically wipe the inside of the hood with the bleach wipe, thoughts bouncing like popcorn inside my mind: Who wore this hood last? What if they have COVID-19? How do I know if it's clean? Do I keep my mask on inside the hood? I spend two minutes wiping the white polyester fabric down and then wait five minutes for it to air out. It never really does. I don the hood, sealing my face inside the fumes, attach the hose to the hood's adaptor and wait for the stale air to circulate through my plastic bubble.

Next comes the thin plastic gown, not silky but not scratchy. Initially cool but soon sticky, unpleasant. Finally, I don another pair of gloves and am ready to moon-walk into the COVID-19 chamber, where the patient is waiting for me.

He was a slim man, lying calmly in the bed. As I spoke, I realized that I could hardly hear him; he projected his voice barely above a whisper that was devoured by my metallic insect. I thought at the time that he had dysphagia from the stroke or from being intubated. I learned later that he had been steadily losing his voice for the past few years after a career as a translator, a curious and undiagnosed condition. I imagined the swift, fluent mind and speech that translators have, how they absorb, swap, and switch words and meanings with such agility. To lose his voice must have been particularly distressing for him.

We didn't say much that first day. He seemed comfortable, had no complaints. I spent less time in the room than it had taken me to get dressed to enter. The next day was largely the same. By the third day, something had changed. He was less interactive, was eating less, refused to work with physical therapy. I called his wife, ashamed that I hadn't called her the first day. She was thrilled to hear from me, and I found myself almost startled by her kindness and positivity. We spoke at length, about his career as a translator, their marriage of over fifty years, their children and grandchildren. Three weeks ago, she had dropped him off at the emergency room, unwell but still walking and talking. Due to the visitor policy, she hadn't been allowed to enter the hospital with him, and she hadn't seen him since.

She told me about a type of origami she had been doing while he was in the hospital. Folded paper cranes are called orizuru—their wings are believed to bear the soul to paradise. I imagined her alone, in a quiet house, folding the paper birds with her hands instead of holding him in her arms. I tried to imagine what three weeks would feel like. She told me the nurses in the ICU had helped them to FaceTime with each other, and she was so grateful. His iPad lay charging on the bedside table, but he wasn't answering anymore. She came to the hospital almost every day with cards from the children and grandchildren. She gave these gifts to the security guard in the lobby and watched as he carried them away.

The next day I wore a face shield over my mask, instead of the PAPR. I walked to his bedside table and there, in fact, were a stack of cards, store-bought and hand-made. I asked if he knew he had gotten so many cards. I couldn't tell by his expression if he had or had not. I asked if it would be okay for me to read his cards to him. He smiled and slightly raised his eyebrows—a clear Yes. And so, I read, one by one, the messages on the cards. Get well soon and You'll be home in no time! The construction paper cards were scrawled upon with crayon; I told him that someone appeared to have drawn him a very scary monster. He laughed, soundlessly. I held the drawing close to him and we agreed that 'monster' was our best guess.

About halfway through this process, an aide entered the room to change his sheets. I didn't realize that he had soiled himself and that she had been getting donned outside the room to complete this task. She worked quickly, glancing at me from time to time. She rolled his thin body onto his side. He did not assist. She exchanged his sheets expertly. His gown was removed, rendering him abruptly naked. I felt an irrational anger toward her for this, this disregard for modesty, the de-personalized efficiency. I wanted to ask her to come back later, but I continued to read. Presently he was clean and gowned and appeared quite content. The aide gave me a curious glance as she left; perhaps wondering about the provider going on and on about children and monsters.

Over the weekend he seemed to retreat inside himself. I spoke with his wife over the phone every day. We discussed discharging him to a skilled nursing facility on Monday. I was hopeful that this would work out; Monday was my last day on service and I didn't want her to start over with yet another faceless provider. She knew, as I did, that she still wouldn't be allowed to see him at the nursing home due to the visitor policy. The virus was gone, but still destroying his life.

We spoke late on Monday morning about plans for the transfer. Something in this conversation, perhaps her probing questions, perhaps the implicit understanding that nothing miraculous would happen at this nursing home, created a subtle tension across the line. I breathed into it. I stepped into this space, as I must, as I have the responsibility and privilege to do. "There is another option," I said. "He could come home, today," I waited. "On hospice." I could hear her exhale. It was as if she had just been waiting for me say it. "I would like that," she said. "Let me talk with the kids."

Things moved very quickly from there. The adult children were in enthusiastic agreement. The case managers were efficient, as always. Suddenly he would be in her home, by 4 pm. Hospice tends to handle this, as with so many other things, exceptionally well. They make a chaotic transition relatively seamless, arriving on site with the bed, setting up the home, educating the family. I called her again that afternoon. She sounded overwhelmed with the logistics and the arrangements, but joyous, energized. I promised her I would call again after he arrived home to make sure everything had gone smoothly. I went on with my day; more patients to see and to admit, families and consultants to call, case management meetings to attend, more donning and doffing. It seemed I was always behind on my notes.

I don't remember what time I got home that evening, or what I did. But I do remember being perched at my countertop bar later that night, hunched over my laptop, a glass of bourbon nearby. I was writing discharge summaries that I hadn't completed at the hospital. My neck and shoulders ached; a headache bloomed behind my eyes. I opened his chart and realized with a jolt of panic that I hadn't called his wife again. Surely he was home by now, it was nearly 9:45 pm. I'll call her tomorrow, I reassured myself. But I had promised. I took a small sip. My cell phone lay on the granite counter; I dialed her number. She answered immediately.

I apologized for calling so late; she didn't seem to mind. I asked her how things had gone, how things were going. She was effusive with praise for the Hospice team. Her husband was home, she said, and once he was settled into the large hospital bed in the living room, she could see that he had visibly relaxed. She was sure that he knew where he was. "He is in the right place," she said. She gushed about their grandchildren, who had rushed to his side and sat holding his hands, petting him and whispering to him. She told me that she hadn't been able to bring them all to the hospital, but she had folded one thousand orizuru—Senbazuru—and she had received her wish: he had come home to her.

Her acceptance and gratitude in the face of so much heartache, where others may have been bitter and resentful, broke something open within me.

All of my efforts to compartmentalize, barricade, and fortify myself crumbled in the presence of her strength. I laid my glasses on the bar and sobbed as soundlessly as he had laughed. I thought of this man, nestled safely in bed beneath a canopy of a thousand paper cranes, basking in the love of his family, like sunrise burning through a dawn of sorrow. The suffering in the world isn't what breaks us; it is the human capacity to love despite the pain that brings us to our knees.

The Start

This essay was written in Atlanta, Georgia

Brittany Ebey
Certified Surgical Technologist
Traveling healthcare professional

That day, you remember the one. I got the text from a friend that we had our first COVID-19 patient in the ICU. I was sitting on the couch. I took a deep breath probably a little deeper than intended and I could tell it rose a small alarm inside of her. She looked over at me and asked. "What's wrong?"

"We have our first patient at the hospital. I won't be coming home for a while once I leave."

I remember that last hug, that last kiss. The tight embrace, the not wanting to let go and at the same time not wanting the fear inside of me to escape into the room but we both felt it.

Walking into work that next day, everything had changed in the few days I had been gone. It almost felt as if one was walking into airport security not a hospital. Check you temp, list of questions, can I see your badge, just a reminder to wear a mask, then it was don't wear a mask (we don't want people getting scared), then back to wear a mask.

I work in Surgery. No procedures to be done, well not enough to sustain the department, so we waited. Daily meetings two to three times a day, all different, all seeming to contradict the last meeting. The fear that could be heard in the director's voice as she delivered the information to us. She tried her best to hide her own fear and frustration yet our questions seemed to attack her and her defensiveness came out and made the fear more evident. After all, it is easy to lead when you know the answers. How hard it must have been to lead when you want to give answers but you don't know them yourself.

Go to room 400 to be "Deployed." That's what they called it when we were sent to other parts of the hospital to help other departments. Mainly the COVID-19 ICUs because who else is better to help and to spot contamination and keep our fellow employees safe than those who do it day in and day out.

I remember the fear in me every day before I went to work, but if I didn't go, who else would be there. The millions of deep breaths taken before entering the unit, before donning my N95, the alarms, what seemed like an endless barrage of codes day after day, hour after hour. The simple things I could do to help bring a patient a glass of water or juice, something to eat, walk into the room with a smile in your eyes pushing aside your own fear so that you can comfort others.

Then the random parades. That seemed weird and unnecessary. The drivebys in a showing of support, the free coffee, donut, etc. We are all just doing our jobs.

Much like the soldier that goes to war for their country, gets injured or dies for their country, they are doing their job. And in both instances when it is all said and done it is as if nothing happened, except it did to us.

The Case

Elizabeth Mitchell, MD

Department of Emergency Medicine ◉ Boston, Massachusetts

It was still early in the scheme of things, as pandemics go. Almost a routine Emergency Department day. COVID was present, but still a vague amorphous threat of unknown facts and presentations. There weren't any medications to treat it with. We were sitting in the eye of the storm, and though we feared what was coming, we were not yet able to feel the force of it. The few patients we had seen so far had been obvious; hypoxic, febrile, in marked respiratory distress requiring intubation, or at least emergent admission to the ICU.

So, I was not really thinking about it when I signed up to see the young woman in room eight on the C side. She was thirty-two years old and healthy. She had recently had a procedure to remove sweat glands in her axilla (armpit), and when she came in her chief complaint was armpit pain. In retrospect of course, it seems obvious that I should have worn a mask and gloves. That all of us should have worn face shields and N95s, head coverings and gowns with every patient. In fact, this became mandatory a short time later. But on this particular day, we were told we should wear surgical masks only with patients having "COVID-like" symptoms.

When I went into room eight after reading the triage note, I was not worried. I took no special precautions. She looked uncomfortable. Her skin flushed. She was anxious. She had a slight temperature, one that would not be considered a fever but was above normal. I pulled up a chair and sat next to her so that we could talk. She told me about going to a specialty clinic for an outpatient surgery because she was always sweating. The surgery had gone well but now the pain had worsened, and she could not get comfortable. Her exam was unrevealing. There were no physical signs of infection, and the surgical sites were healing well. Her breathing seemed a bit too rapid, but I attributed it to her anxiety and discomfort. Her oxygen levels were fine. We checked some labs, which showed inflammation but were otherwise normal. We called the clinic where she had had the procedure and were reassured when we were told that inflammation and pain even after two weeks was normal. The procedure had not been a long one and there were no intra-operative complications. So, finding no acute problem, we treated her with a non-steroidal pain medicine and explained that everything appeared to be normal, and she was discharged.

The next day I was at work again, and midway through my shift, Lily, the nurse I had worked with the day before, rushed up to me.

"Do you remember the woman with the armpit pain?" Lily was an older nurse who had worked in the hospital for almost forty years.

"Of course," I said.

"You won't believe it," she said. "She's at another hospital intubated in the ICU with COVID!"

I felt my world turn slowly around, as I took this in. I felt unmoored, nauseous, incredulous. How could I have missed it? How was that possible? Should I have seen it? And suddenly I felt it, the amorphous beast of COVID had morphed into something much worse. It was like an alien that could take any form and infect anyone, young or old. It wasn't just the elderly. It wasn't just fever, cough, and shortness of breath. It was anything. It was a thirty-two-year-old with painful armpits who ended up on a ventilator in an ICU. It could take any of us. I had been without PPE. Was I next? Was Lily? Was I going to get sick and die? I felt ill. I finished my shift in a state of disbelief.

That was the last time that I would not wear PPE with every patient, on every shift, for well over a year. That was the start of what would be a time unlike any other.

Mask

Michael Schmitz, DO
Emergency Medicine ⚙ Biddeford, Maine

Green
Thick with microfilaments
Cupping my nose and mouth
Not quite smothering
Hopefully protecting
Muffling not just my words,
But my timing, cadence, patience and smile
Forcing inhalation and exhalation
Through the conscious work of breathing

Counteracted only by my gloved hand
Resting upon a naked forearm
A meager attempt to make up the chasm
In the boundaries of our communication
Trying to say:
"I've got you"
And
"It's going to be okay"

Defining Moments

Margaret Lamkin, DO
Staff Physician ⊛ Central Alabama Montgomery VA Clinic
Montgomery, Alabama

There I was at the beach house, March 2020, sitting on the grey sofa next to my mom, in "lock down mode" issued by the Alabama governor. We watched the news of hospital overcrowding in New York City, learned of increasing COVID deaths, saw portable morgues and makeshift clinics—like watching a horror movie or reading a sci-fi novel. A call was issued across the nation for health care workers to assist in the pandemic. Physicians, nurses and others were interviewed boarding planes, doffing in PPE from head to toe, honored as heroes by national media. I was in between jobs; I had been offered a job in March, but it got delayed due to clinic closure. Furloughed from my part time, urgent care work, my only "service" in this time of need was as a weekend hospitalist in Greenville, AL once a month, where we had yet to see any COVID cases.

I felt rested, yet restless, tired yet bored, helpless as if watching the world through a window. I wanted to help yet I was scared. All of a sudden, an email appeared on my phone- "Can you leave tomorrow and work in a COVID field hospital in Atlanta?" Yes, I thought. I'm trained, available, and willing. I'll go.

My mom, however, was terrified and begged me not to go. She said she was certain I'd contract COVID if I went to Atlanta and worked with COVID patients. However, I had to go. It seemed like my decision to enter medical school as a second career culminated in this opportunity to serve. I made a hasty decision, emailed back, made travel arrangements, and arrived two days later.

Whenever I called my mom from Atlanta, I described all of my safety measures: how I was wiping down the hotel room with Clorox wipes—even the doorknobs, faucet, telephone, remote control. I set up a "clean bed" to be used only for sleeping after showering, and a "dirty bed" I could sit on or put my stuff on before I showered. Nightly, I came in and stripped inside the door, placing my scrubs in a laundry bag for washing by the hotel.

I first entered the facility, the Georgia World Congress Center, in the cold zone, not knowing anyone. Later I met my team and learned stories about how other physicians felt called to serve. I received extensive training on how to dress in PPE; a safety officer always monitoring donning and doffing when entering the "hot zone"—the area where patients were housed. We were allotted only 4-hour increments in the hot zone during which time we could not eat, use the restroom, or leave. I diligently wore my N95 mask like a second skin in the hot zone, and I always made sure I wore other masks when in the "cold" zone.

Daily I expected my own symptoms to appear. I wondered: "Do I have a sore throat, is that a headache?" I waited for my shifts, anticipated a day off, and held on for tragedy, uncertainty, disease, and death. I met new people, shared worries, fears, and doubts, learned new practices about COVID and treated more patients. I walked outside for exercise in Centennial Park, passing the CNN building, the Chick-fil-A, through the park, filled with homeless people, streets deserted, restaurants closed.

I gained confidence. I reassured my mother. I felt like I was a part of something bigger than myself. I was no longer afraid, knowing that COVID was a life-changing/defining moment.

Like going to war, I signed up and served until my time was done. I returned home.

Dialogue

Joanne Wilkinson, MD, MSc

Medical Director ⊛ Family Care Center ⊛ Pawtucket RI

Mom, do you have a minute for a question?

I will in a second honey, I'm just taking off my gloves and everything. Okay. Can you hear me? No? Let me move over to the window, the cell phone reception isn't great on this floor. Okay, now?

Mom, I'm trying to do my science homework and they want us to hand it in by one. Can I ask you a question about cells?

Yeah, totally, I know all about cells. It's a good thing you have me for this homework, because I know more about cells than all the other moms.

Is cytoplasm a liquid or a solid?

Well, that's a good question. We don't really know, because no one can see it. But we think it's a thick liquid, like Jell-O.

Mom, I'm glad you brought that up, because they want us to make a model of a cell using Jell-O.

What, like now?

Yeah, the instructions say 'Have a parent help you with this' and we're supposed to use Jell-O, and cut-up fruit and stuff to be the like, parts of the cell?

And that's due today? Like, in an hour?

Yeah.

Honey, there's no way. I have four more patients to see here, I won't even be home in an hour. Do you want me to email your teacher?

No, it's okay, I just won't hand it in.

But that's not fair, Boo. Are all the other parents really at home doing this?

I don't know. It seems like they are.

Honey.

It's okay, mom. I know you have to work.

Honey, I feel bad about this. Could we get a one-day extension?

I don't know—Hey mom?

Yes lovey?

Are you wearing your mask?

Yes, why, can you not hear me?

No, I want to make sure you're wearing it all the time. Don't take it off, okay?

PART II
Relentless Service

INTRODUCTION

Kerry L. Malawista, Ph.D.

THE THINGS THEY CARRY PROJECT ATTRACTED frontline workers eager to find their voice, to articulate all they have experienced, and to pronounce: this happened to me. Workshops provided the physical and psychological space for healthcare workers to translate difficult emotions into words. Expressing trauma in language—whether verbal or written—can be psychologically beneficial. When done in a manageable way, writing about distressing life events not only promotes emotional and physical health but also fosters a sense of hope.

In this way, writing and therapy have much in common as tools for examining life. Either may start by replaying hurtful events, the *"what happened?"* But that is only one part of the process. The work can't stop there. The initial writing must lead to mulling over and thoughtful reflection, a chance to say, *this is how I understand what happened to me.* Like therapy, writing requires questioning, alongside thoughtful reflection—an orchestrated re-imagining, re-working and shaping of memories and experiences that explain ourselves to ourselves, allowing for change and re-vision. And both milieus' offer the powerful element of another person witnessing what has happened to us, offering connection over isolation.

Memory is often a bodily experience, needing to be translated in to sensory terms and feelings. One way to access deeper feelings is to hone the details of a recollection. All art, whether writing, music or painting, is about paying attention; thus, workshop leaders encouraged group members to engage as many senses as they can and with as much specificity as they could muster. I recall my daughter, Sarah, a painter, telling me, "Mom, look up, the sky is not just one color. Really look closely. See there is some crimson, violet and yellow, not just blue. Nothing is just one color."

The same is true for writing as it is for painting. It's not just a stethoscope you hold against a patient's chest. There is the *lub-dub, lub-dub,* you hear, along with the cold and sterile feeling of the metal in your hands. There are, too, the odors you notice in the room—your own breath inside the mask, the antiseptic of hospital sanitizer, or the flowers resting next to the patient's bed.

Nurse Susan Perron lists the never-ending array of medications at her disposal—Fentanyl, Propofol, Versed, and Nimbex. The reader senses the weight of her decisions: Will the medication she dispenses heal or harm her patient? Cycling through her mind is the constant refrain, "Am I enough?" Susan leaves the nightshift not knowing if her patient will be alive or dead when she returns the next day. They were trained to save people and now they are watching them die.

Writing allowed frontline workers to get in touch with feelings and thoughts they didn't know existed before they picked up the pen. In all of the particulars, it is not about the quality of the writing, but the *process* of writing.

Dipa Saha, a pediatrician, copes with the day-in-day-out of death and devastation by dividing her day into small increments– the seconds, minutes, and hours–snippets of time. Similarly, Joanne Wilkinson, a family care doctor, gets through her day by focusing "on one job at a time, one crisis at a time, one patient at a time." Like organizing a life, organizing our thoughts in writing focuses us and makes us hopeful and feel a bit more in control.

Our group members found support not only in writing but also in reading their pieces aloud to one another, or if not wanting to read, telling the group what they wrote about. Participants found they shared the same language—the language of medicine—transcending age, sex, race, and education level. Many teared up when sharing their words or listening to another tell their story. Participants could reflect back to the writer what they heard. Being listened to is a transformative experience, one that gives permission to heal.

Uncharted Territory

Susan Perron, RN, BSN

Medical ICU Vanderbilt Medical Center ❖ Nashville, Tennessee

"This is scaring me," I told my nurse practitioner, as I continued to turn up my patient's sedation, steadily climbing past the pump's guardrails.

"Is this safe?" I whispered to myself, hands trembling.

She looked back at me through the patient's door and replied over my respirator's walkie, "Yes, this is scary. We are in uncharted territory; there is no instruction manual for this."

Fentanyl, Propofol, Versed, and Nimbex, all reaching maximum dosages as I continued to titrate up. I looked at my patient, strapped to an ECMO machine, trached, vented, and hooked to countless wires monitoring vital signs, while wrapped up in a warming blanket. And this was not just any ECMO patient, but one who needed a double or "butterfly" ECMO circuit, which graced his body like wings, to keep him alive.

In street speak, ECMO (extracorporeal membrane oxygenation) is a device that can bypass blood going to the lungs and pumps it into a machine that filters out CO_2 while delivering oxygen to the blood; then it sends the filtered blood back into a major artery to circulate around the body. The hope is that this will give the lungs time to heal. It's usually a grim prognosis by the time a COVID-19 patient ends up on ECMO and grimmer if it's a butterfly ECMO. A simple turn or cough could cause the patient's oxygen levels to plummet, and there is no guarantee that their oxygen levels would recover, no matter what medical miracle we perform.

"Hell," I thought, "just looking at him could cause him to code."

I could feel the droplets of perspiration run down my back. My green scrubs were drenched under the layers of blue plastic shielding me from the virus. Everything just stuck to me. The cool air from my respirator, my saving grace, fanned my sweaty face. COVID-19 is such a heart-breaking disease. Even if your patient beats COVID-19, their lungs may never recover, causing their ultimate demise. Working in a place like the COVID-19 ICU will test you mentally, physically, and spiritually on a daily basis. This case was no exception.

My charge nurse knocked on my window. The patient's wife is on the phone for an update. They live almost three hours away and she is now the sole caregiver for their children.

What do I say? How do I tell someone their loved one is not doing well? How do I avoid giving them false hope? I tell them the truth; I keep to the facts. I summarize my assessment, changes in ECMO settings, drip rates, recent labs, and goals for the evening. Sometimes my only goal is to keep the patient stable until the next shift shows up. It's grim. Then I hear her sweet voice over the receiver telling me that God is looking out for us, and she has all faith in my abilities as a nurse. I'm glad someone does, I think to myself, as I fight back the urge to cry.

I get off the phone and doubt creeps in. What am I doing here? I ask myself, Am I enough? What have I gotten myself into? Am I really helping people? Am I really making a difference? After my shifts in the COVID-19 ICU, I leave with the sick feeling of defeat. It's hard when you see so many of your patients die. You start second-guessing your every action, decision, and intervention. I began doubting my convocation that led me to become a nurse. I call this phenomenon the silent killer of health care careers.

I look around and stare at all the handmade drawings, get well cards, and family pictures adorning my patient's walls, a reminder that cocooned within this nest of wires and medical equipment is a well-loved human being. Praying, I snap out of my funk and spring back into action, telling my doubts, WE are not doing this tonight. For the rest of the shift, I focus on the here and now. I focus what I can do for my patient in this moment.

As 7 a.m. approaches, the day shift, fresh from their showers and night sleep, shuffle in to get a report. My patient is still alive, sedated, and relatively stable. I consider this a win in my book. I did the best I could, I told myself. The rest is in God's hands. As I leave the COVID-19 ICU, I try not to look back at my patient, as it is often the last time I will see them alive. It's too painful. I make it out to the parking garage and climb into my Corolla. Jeff Buckley's "Hallelujah" plays over the radio. I sigh; exhausted, I kick back my seat and close my eyes for five short minutes.

Weeks pass. I try not to think of my previous patients—I just neatly compartmentalize my work life so that I can carry on. Oftentimes, I have no idea what happens to my patients once they leave my care. As an ICU nurse, that is one of the luxuries I have. On this particular day, it was my turn to cycle back into the "normal" medical ICU, giving me a much-needed break from COVID-19. As I passed by the charge nurse's desk to get my assignment, I peered into a nearby room. Looking back at me was my Butterfly Man. He waved. I smiled ear to ear.

Snippets

Dipanwita Saha, MD, FAAP
Champion for Quality and Safety, PM Pediatrics
Columbia, Maryland

My work is divided into snippets: snippets of time, snippets of people, snippets of pain, snippets of happiness, relief, anxiety, and fear. I never quite get more, or I never quite get less. Working clinically during the pandemic comes with an underlying foundation of distance and devastation, like an intense movie playing on the TV in the background while you are working or making dinner. You want to pay attention, but you also want to live your life.

That day I was already tired, not physically but emotionally. I was counting down the hours; I texted Michael at home: 2 more hours. Looking at my wristwatch, had it really only been 7 minutes since the last time I checked the time?

My nurse told me about a father and daughter that had checked in on the "clean" side, the side that doesn't have anything to do with COVID-19. The dad told me that he had noticed his 2-year old's abdomen looked swollen, but that she had been happy and herself, with no other symptoms.

Constipation, I thought to myself. Or the dad had felt something anatomically normal but new to him. I went in with my reassurance stance. I felt around her abdomen. It was large, hard, unmissable. I took a long breath. How do I tell this little girl's father, this is likely the start of a very long road during extraordinary times?

My nurse knocks on the door, "Sorry, doctor, can you please come look at this patient?" I go outside: a child's face had been bitten by a dog. Everyone was hysterical: the child was screaming; the mom was sobbing. How do I divide my attention? How do I lend my empathy equally to two traumatizing experiences? I go slow and take a deep breath. Only 20 minutes to go of my shift, but I will be here longer, trying to help as I can, these two-family snippets I was given today.

I come home 1.5 hours after my shift ended. Michael asks, what happened? Nothing, love, some last-minute patients. I shower, my mind, body, and soul drained, and I close my eyes in bed, trying to shut it out.

Lessons

Sarah A. MD

Infectious Disease Physician ◉ New York, NY

Every aspect of my life was affected by the pandemic: my sleep-wake cycle was interrupted by pages, my commute on the New York City subway was infused with fear, my clinical duties lengthened and became more exhaustive, even the food I was able to access changed, and became scarcer. The bustling, busy New York City—famous in movies and TV shows—the New York that has enthralled the world, suddenly felt empty and deserted. I could count on one hand the people now traipsing the streets of Time Square, and with Broadway closed, and international travel nonexistent, why would people visit?

The virus was certainly in New York City long before we were able to detect it. In the initial days, in March 2020, criteria to test for COVID, as dictated by the Department of Health, was strict: patients had to have recently traveled from Wuhan or been in communication with someone who had. We now know that the majority of US cases in fact originated from Europe. Like so much of the US's management of the early pandemic, those guidelines had limitations and were not protective. Once testing became more available, it became clear that I was in a COVID hotspot.

In March 2020, I was the sole fellow in the Infectious Disease clinic at Elmhurst Hospital in Queens, New York, which was highlighted by the *New York Times* and other media outlets as the "epicenter of COVID-19." During the first days of my rotation at Elmhurst, pre-pandemic, I was consulted on bread-and-butter infectious disease cases: multidrug-resistant bacterial infections, tuberculosis, bloodstream infections etc. However, as testing for COVID became available, my focus and that of the entire hospital quickly became one hundred percent on COVID cases. I was inundated with questions from medical teams, surgical teams, nurses, and everyone I encountered when walking the now-feared hospital corridors.

I barely had time to keep up with the news. My friends all seemed more up-to-date with the latest political speeches and updates on the numbers of cases. I fell into a routine of commuting on the subway in fear, while trying not to touch any surface or come in too close contact with anyone at work. Coming home required an hour-long process of disrobing and decontamination in the hallway of my now-deserted Manhattan walkup.

Oddly, within what felt like a matter of days, I was treated differently. Throngs of people applauded essential workers each night at 7 pm. Garbagemen saluted me as I walked in my scrubs. Like most traumatic events, the experience of those early days of surging cases at Elmhurst Hospital felt disjointed.

I think back to first time I donned full personal protective equipment. A patient on steroids presented with shortness of breath, requiring a non-rebreather (a device that gives maximal oxygen). My attending told me, "I'm sure this is PCP because he's on steroids, not COVID, but let's check just in case. Let's wear all the protective gear to practice donning and doffing." Under the illusion of an alternate diagnosis, I calmly put on all the gear. As I was about to enter the room, a nurse called out to me, "Hey, doc! Don't forget the booty covers!" I thanked him and covered my shoes with another layer of protection. The following day, the patient deteriorated, requiring intubation. We started broad spectrum antibiotics and monitored him closely. And then, 6 days later, to our astonishment, his SARS CoV-2 PCR test returned positive.

My mind rushed to various thoughts from the recesses of my brain: six days had passed and I felt okay. Was I outside of the incubation period? I just did not know.

And then it happened again. This time, I wasn't protected. A patient with a foot infection continued to spike fevers. My team thought that the patient's infection required further surgical debridement. As his course continued, the patient complained of a cough, and a CT scan the surgeons ordered returned with a Radiology read of "likely COVID pneumonia." I had been seeing this patient daily, without any mask at all. There was not yet any hospital or official recommendation to wear a mask. That moment of realizing the positive COVID diagnosis seared crisply in my brain. I wondered if I had been exposed to something that would result in my death.

And then, alarmingly, I wondered if I may already have the virus, and may have spread it to patients at Elmhurst Hospital as an asymptomatic carrier. This thought was unbearable. Did I give it to the 85-year-old abuela awaiting her hospital discharge, or to the patient recovering from an infected wound, or what about the patient who already had tuberculosis?

I soon realized that I would never feel comfortable seeing my family again. Too much felt at stake. One overextended hug or cough could lead to me transmitting something lethal and disabling. My mind and body felt numb. And there was no obvious or clear solution to resolving how I felt or what consequences may arise.

Because of an inadequate supply of personal protective equipment, it became clear that we could not see every patient on our service. We were re-using our N95 masks, and as an Infectious Disease consult service, we felt that using up protective gear would be irresponsible—that the gear should go to the primary teams and nurses who saw patients daily. While I knew this policy was the best for the primary teams and staff in the hospital, it made me feel disconnected. I read charts daily of patients rapidly decompensating; becoming intubated; having a cardiac arrest and dying. It felt that every patient's fate was inevitable. I could not help but cry as I read notes from the chaplains and team members, planning end of life care. Harder, too, was reading the charts of patients in their thirties.

Oddly, as an Infectious Disease specialist, I felt partly responsible for the scale of deaths. Teams turned to me for answers, and I felt their stinging disappointment when I had little to share. When they called me at 3 am for a rapidly decompensating patient, and my only answer was to give supportive care, I felt like a massive failure. That I was failing myself, my patients, and the residents who turned to me.

Months later, in June 2020, I went to a clinic for an employee COVID antibody test. To my astonishment, the word "negative" flashed before my screen. I sighed in relief that I had not worsened the pandemic by asymptomatically spreading the virus. However, in the same moment I lamented that I did not have immunity. The possibility of later contracting the virus and becoming sick, or asymptotically or pre-symptomatically spreading it to others, remained possible.

On the last day of my rotation at Elmhurst Hospital in April 2020, I walked slowly through the plexiglass doors, brimming with feelings of both reprieve from an intense work environment, and sadness to leave the patients that had dominated my life. I paused in front of the hospital: before me was a large sign, crafted by a local artist that said, "THANK YOU" in bold, bright blue letters. I surveyed the public park near the hospital and past the blue letters, and I thought about all the community members who had played sports there and performed cultural dances and tai chi. As residents of the most diverse zip code in the world, the patients at Elmhurst Hospital are a microcosm of that world. Within Queens alone, 138 languages are spoken. In pre-pandemic times, a walk down the street from the hospital featured cuisines from all over the globe, signs in multiple languages, and a bustling community.

The patients of Elmhurst Hospital are people who know great pain: they know the pain of exile from their native countries, the pain of economic disadvantage, and of unequal treatment and inequalities in their care. Yet even in the hardest times, these patients showed unthinkable gratitude. When I stumbled through patient encounters with imperfect Spanish, they told me they were so relieved to talk to someone who spoke their language. When I told them that I didn't know if their COVID test would be positive or negative, that I didn't know when the test would come back, that I didn't even know what this disease we heard about on TV meant, they listened to me with understanding and kindness.

Since the pandemic's early days, I have returned to Elmhurst Hospital's Infectious Disease clinic.

As I discuss patient's treatment plans for non-COVID related concerns, the patients tell me how they had fevers in March but stayed at home, and how their COVID antibodies are now positive. They extend their hand to me and say "Gracias a Dios" that they are now healthy. The Elmhurst community carries on. They have affection and belief in me as their health care provider, despite having seen unthinkable lows and despair.

In the midst of a pandemic, all of life feels vivid and intense. In those moments, it is unclear when the intensity will wane and run its course; it is difficult to think of any end at all. Fortunately, New York City's cases dramatically improved with social distancing, masking, and thankfully efficacious and safe vaccines.

The pandemic showed me that under duress, our experiences become the most up-to-date information that we have. That what we have to offer when there are no solutions and no cures, when the advice we have is rapidly overturned, that when nothing seems clear at all, our kindness and humanity for one another is what matters most. That looking out for our colleagues and our patients' wellness rewards us all. When leadership and treatments are not available, love, connection, and affirmation endure.

Thank You for Your Service

Joanne Wilkinson, MD, MSc
Medical Director ◉ Family Care Center
New England Primary & Specialty Care ◉ Pawtucket, RI

When it started, I knew before everyone else how bad it could be. I told my family in mid-February that we were done eating out, and that my dad and stepmother should stop going to church. I had endless Zoom calls and conference calls trying to plan our clinic's response, how we would deal with the walk-ins who had cold symptoms, how we would conserve the gowns and gloves. I wore the same surgical mask for six weeks at the beginning.

Every morning, I woke up early and put my glasses on and brought the phone up to my face to read the coronavirus numbers in the state and how many vents were in use. I feared getting sick: the fever, the cough, the wishful thinking that maybe it was allergies, the worry about who would take care of my daughter, the ambulance, the worried colleagues looking at me through their face shields, and then the iPad coming into the room so that I could try to find something to say to my daughter before I was paralyzed and intubated. My stomach was permanently clenched.

I focused on one job at a time, one crisis at a time, one patient at a time. I stripped off my clothes every day in the back entryway of our house and threw them immediately in the washer. The emails came from my daughter's school endlessly: she wasn't on the last 5 minutes of the Math zoom, she had a glitch turning in her online reading log, she looked sad in zoom advisor meetings. She was home alone while I worked in a respiratory tent, texting me questions like "Is cytoplasm liquid or solid?" while I was trying to hear patients' lungs in the wind and rain coursing through the parking lot.

One day a patient stopped as they were leaving the tent. "Thank you for your service," they said to me matter-of-factly. That was all. Mine is not a military family. My dad was in the National Guard during Vietnam and often tells the story that of three units in the state, his was the only one not called up. He considers this lucky and so do I. On my mom's side, no one was in the military. My grandfather was too young for World War 1 and too old for World War 2. The others were all girls.

Mine is not a military family but I was tempted to salute. Somehow at that moment, it was enough.

My Southside Chicago Nightshift Staff

Melissa Vargas, MPH, MSN, RN
Emergency Department ❋ Southside Chicago, Illinois

A night in the life of the emergency room is never the same twice. Depending on the day and hour, we could have a tranquil waiting room with most of our patients being courteous and understanding as we wait for their CT scan results, or we could be dodging verbal threats as we tell our patients the cafeteria is closed and all we have are turkey sandwiches on white bread, with mayo, if they are lucky. My point being, there is no monotony, which is both a treat and a curse. Yet my main drive to return to this hospital every single shift has nothing to do with the hospital itself, and everything to do with the staff I accidently fell in with, and found a home with, almost three years ago.

The beauty (and some would argue, drawback) of working in a 27-bed ER is that you see the same colleagues, day in and day out, and without meaning to, you get to know everything about them: from their hometowns to their family vacations, and of course, if they are team Sox or team Cubs. All the time spent starting BiPAPs on patients with the respiratory team, helping the environmental service (EVS) team clean up after a code blue with medical equipment on every counter and corner of the floor, and digging through an overdose patient's pockets with registration to try to find an ID has led to comradery, and luckily for me, strong friendships. Our shared experiences after cleaning a bed-bound patient with incessant diarrhea with a team of our nurses and techs—or taking turns answering the call light for our frequent flyer, alcoholic patient, only to tell him for the 30th time he cannot leave until he has sobered up—have led us to earn each other's respect, all the while helping our shifts run efficiently with arguably a little too much laughter for the amount of dark situations we see.

This is why our ER flow works. This is how we are able to get our patients the care they come for, with only 4 nurses, 2 techs, and 1 physician at times, and why people prefer us in the southside area to some of our nearby hospital alternatives. This is how we were able to treat a multiple-gunshot-wound victim who drove himself to the hospital and transfer him within 45 minutes to the nearest trauma hospital. Everyone did their part: the 2 nurses in the room started IVs and gave pain meds, while monitoring vital signs; the tech got the patient's EKG and glucose checked; the unit secretary paged trauma centers to find a bed; the x-ray tech took images to help the doctor place a chest tube; the EVS cleaned up the pools of blood after the patient left, and the room looked like it was the first time it had ever received a patient.

All of this is why I go back, after sleeping through most of the "normal" day, only to get up to pack my daily 32 ounces of coffee, banana, little oranges, and avocado toast for another night of unpredictable but organized chaos.

Tricky Decisions

Sarah A., MD
Infectious Disease ☀ New York, NY

Dr. Jones* knocked on my door. I was inside the fellows' room, on the 6th floor of Elmhurst Hospital. Normally, my door would be open, ready for visitors to stop by to say hello or for residents to ask quick questions about antibiotics. As an Infectious Disease fellow, I often described myself as an "antibiotic doctor" who helped teams treat challenging infections caused by multidrug- resistant bacteria. However, the World Health Organization had just declared a global pandemic days before, and one by one, every patient I had seen tested positive for COVID-19. I now walked past camera crews as I entered the hospital, as the New York Times had just shown footage of bodies being disposed of into trucks outside the hospital. The Emergency Room was teeming with patients waiting outside for blocks, waiting to get a coveted COVID test. The small, warm, community hospital with patients from countries all over the world, where I had become an expert in utilizing translation services and perfecting my medical Spanish, was now in the center of a media storm as virus transmission roared through the community and overwhelmed the hospital.

Even patients I had seen who presented without respiratory complaints— who came in for diabetic foot ulcers, necrotizing fasciitis, strokes—they all tested positive for the virus, too.

At that point, I had been exposed without a mask several times—in the

---

preceding weeks, the thought was that masks would not protect us, so initially I, too, did not wear one. Even worse, I told friends who turned to me for advice to also spare themselves the hassle of masking up.

Dr. Jones knocked again, and I grabbed my N95 and surgical mask from next to my desk, the surface still glistening from its most recent Clorox scrub down. Atop the sparkling surface was a bottle of study drug: hydroxychloroquine vs placebo. I had enrolled in a study for health care workers exposed to COVID-19, and the University of Minnesota had sent me a bottle overnight. I had still not decided whether or not to take the study drug, whether it was hydroxychloroquine or placebo. I feared the fate of some of my patients who had developed fatal arrhythmias on the medication, a drug that we touted as our only hope.

Dr. Jones stood in front of me, her short bob combed neatly, and a smile could be discerned even from her double set of masks. But her eyes, they looked tired.

"Sarah, any patients you recommend for Toci?" she was using medical slang for the interleukin-6 inhibitor, Tocilizumab, which we were just learning might help control the inflammatory response of COVID-19. She continued, "I heard you might have a young pregnant patient with a few kids at home."

She was referring to a patient who had been on the verge of intubation for several days. She was in her thirties, and in her third trimester. She had no past medical conditions— information that the public often demanded when discussing any serious COVID-19 disease. It always felt that a mention of "diabetes" or "hypertension" might send waves of relief, with the subtle, unfair belief that serious illness was more acceptable in persons with some risk factors.

The nurses said that the patient had begged to be intubated overnight because she had a hard time breathing. But the ICU did not intubate her, nor did we advocate for intubation, because at that moment in time, none of the patients that had been intubated at Elmhurst had had their breathing tube removed—they had all died.

My friends and colleagues hammer-texted my phone daily; they thought New York City, with its messy subways and crowded housing was some sort of exemplary case of a city primed for virus transmission. A few months later, these same friends would find themselves in my position—watching as their hospital gift shops were converted to patient rooms as hospital systems became overwhelmed.

I read fervently on Tocilizumab and was not sure if it could be given to a pregnant patient. I called the drug company, and the representative was surprised that we had started giving interleukin-6 inhibitors for COVID. She cited 500 cases of women who had been exposed to Tocilizumab for rheumatologic indications, who were unknowingly pregnant at the time. The incidence of birth defects was not higher than the background rate in this group, although there was not yet any published literature on this. But from what I had seen of the virus, and what I observed of this young mother's condition, it seemed like there was no other option than to prescribe Tocilizumab. We advocated for an early cesarean section, and the baby was born prematurely.

Both mother and child survived.

Will We Ever See Her Again?

Owen Lee-Park, MD
Resident ● Emergency Medicine
George Washington Hospital ● Washington, DC

The husband stood still next to J, holding her hand and standing ever so still, with his small frame, stooped over, tears in his eyes. "I'm right here, it's going to be okay. I won't leave you."

The husband then pulled me aside into a corner and whispered, "Can you tell me what the visitation policy is going to be for my wife..." he said as he looked around to make sure his wife couldn't hear him through the loud BiPAP machine. "...with her COVID diagnosis?"

Reflecting off his eyes were so many years of memories shared together—the deep love and care, and the endless fear, reaching out for an answer. Reaching for anything hopeful. I will ask the ICU doctor what the ICU unit policy is, I said, as each unit is different. I will try my best, knowing that it is probably unlikely that he or any of his family members will get to see her during this hospitalization.

"My wife... Her father died here in this hospital last year, at the beginning of the pandemic. None of us could visit him because of the strict visitation policy at the beginning of the pandemic. Once he got admitted, we never got to see or say goodbye to him. That's why I'm whispering. We're... she's still so traumatized. That's why we're all, our kids..." his phone lighting up again for the third time. A frantic, desperate ring from the caller "Daughter."

"I will find out. I will try my best. I will come back and let you know. It's going to be okay. Let's take it one step at a time. We can't look too far ahead. Just one step at a time, just this present moment. The fact that she's not intubated, and instead on BiPAP, that's a good sign... I... will be back."

I stepped out of the room. I spoke to the intensivist, pleaded with him if it would be possible.

It would not be possible, it turns out, unless the patient wasn't able to communicate for herself. It's unfortunate, but that's the rule right now, the intensivist said with palpable sadness hidden under his gentle but stern voice, as if he's had to say the same thing multiple times just today.

I stood outside J's room. Her husband on the phone, still holding on to her weak, clammy hand. Because of her immunocompromised condition, she hadn't been able to get vaccinated, only her husband and their children had.

The husband couldn't fathom how she could've contracted COVID. They were so careful, he said. They never left the house except for her medical appointments and always wore masks. With tears in his eyes, the husband kept asking the question out loud, "How? Why?"

She had done everything right. She would've gotten her vaccine at her first chance if it wasn't for her immune compromised health condition.

I wept in my car ride back home. How? Why?

Travel Bag

Sandra Beirne, MD
Physician Rural ◈ New Mexico

We warmed the tips of our fingers in our armpits, fully aware that the biting morning would soon warm into a just-beyond pleasantly warm afternoon, and we would be shedding layers that would drape over the back of every metal folding chair in our makeshift clinic. All COVID-19 triaging care had been moved outside, indefinitely. It was kind of nice to work outside; a silver lining to the tragedy that was playing out in the building 20 feet behind me.

I kept thinking, "When does a doctor ever get to work outside?" and tried to enjoy the fresh air and the views out to the distant mesas, using those good thoughts to distract from the pressing anxiety of May 2020. The pleasantness of outside was punctuated by activity at the helicopter pad, about 100 feet down the ED entrance ramp road, as patients were transferred out to any tertiary hospital within a 400-mile range that would take them. The flight crew wheeling an immobile patient down the bumpy concrete to the waiting chopper made avoidant thoughts of pleasant outdoor work difficult. Those were actually the luckier patients, the ones the team thought might survive with stepped-up care. Many of the patients admitted that spring for COVID-19 infection didn't get transferred out or discharged.

It was the family of one of those patients who pulled up in front of our outdoor workspace that morning as we warmed our fingertips. They had already spoken to the ED triage nurse stationed up the road, but they pulled in and parked and then nothing happened. Typically, a nurse approached the car and got more information from the patient on their needs and then started a documentation sheet and identified a provider who would see the patient and evaluate them. But this car just stayed parked and no one approached them. There appeared to be 4 or 5 people in the sedan, distributed between the back and front seats. Occasionally, the driver would briefly glance our way, but still, nothing happened. I asked a few of the nurses what was needed for this car but got only shrugs and averted eyes. After 15 or so minutes of waiting for someone else to figure out what needed to be done, and knowing we were going to need that space for other patients, I walked over to the car. The young woman in the driver's seat rolled down the window and quietly told me they were there to pick up items from her father who had passed away that morning. The air felt sucked out of the space, replaced by heavy, dense grief. No one in the car cried, no one smiled, no one even looked up.

Finding the bag of the recently decreased man's items was frustratingly difficult, and I returned to the patiently waiting car full of his loved ones and handed the clear plastic bag to the driver. The young woman was quiet but inhaled sharply when I handed her the bag full of clothes and shoes that her father had worn into the hospital. What would they do with these things? What do you do with the shoes of someone who died suddenly? The clothes? Especially the last things they wore alive. And how is this clear trash bag of things their only goodbye? He was alive outside our hospital, he entered alone, and he died in there, alone, with the only things left of him, their only goodbye, this flimsy trash bag and the items he had on his body when he entered. How would they ever be able to get a place of peace with his death when it was hidden away and he died without his family by his side?

I fumbled through my own tears, saying the usual condolence phrases, and she thanked me for caring for her father and left with her family. I didn't do anything for him. I never met him, I didn't deserve that thanks. I wanted to chase the car and tell her that as a pediatrician, I have felt helpless, inept, sitting by as my adult-provider colleagues and respiratory therapists, nurses, health techs, and housekeepers did everything they could to stop death for the influx of COVID-19 infected patients, and for those they couldn't, provide a respectful transition from life. And that was before vaccine protection, before we understood the details of COVID-19 transmission. Those staff worked all night long for her father, and the many other patients like him; they worked night after night, away from their families, and worried about spreading infection to them when they finally did go home to them. I needed to give this thanks to them, who so profoundly deserved it. But the COVID ward, and those who worked on it, was unreachable, a sealed-off world full of providers overwhelmed with sickness and death and not checking emails. So I mumbled it to the nearby family medicine docs working outside with me that day, likely none of whom had ever met this man either, and we moved on to the next patient who pulled up.

PART III

Promises We Can't Keep

INTRODUCTION

Kerry L. Malawista, Ph.D.

BY THE CLOSE OF 2021, MORE THAN 800,000 PEOPLE HAVE died of COVID-19 in the United States and 5.4 million worldwide, each death sending reverberations through family, friends, and the medical community caring for the individuals. Frontline workers describe the pain, sorrow, and helplessness of witnessing countless deaths. Added to their burden was carrying the loss of patients who died alone, without their loved ones nearby.

While death is a discrete event in time, coping with the aftermath is an intensely personal process that evolves over months, even years. While there are many theories on the trauma of loss, no two people grieve in the same way, nor is there a right or wrong way to grieve, yet for each of us it is a wound that requires time and attention to heal. And although it is often not helpful to pathologize loss and grief, or view it as a mental illness, it is notable that in 2021, during the pandemic, the Diagnostic and Statistical Manual of Mental Disorders (DSM) added the diagnosis of prolonged grief disorder, or P.G.D, to their diagnostic taxonomy.

ER doctor Diane Birnbaumer writes about the regret and guilt she feels after promising a patient, "We're not going to let you die," a promise she can't keep. She describes the burning, lingering feeling of failure and the ghosts "whose lives intersected. In these life-altering, terrible moments."

For many healthcare workers, a death may remain stuck in their mind for months, even years. They may be left continually questioning their competency as a nurse or doctor. Did they make a mistake? Was it their fault? What more could they have done? Promises not kept by healthcare workers who are supposed to heal the sick but are helpless in the face of the virus, lack of supplies, lack of knowledge, quarantine and solitude.

The helplessness and sadness at not being able to save patients is compounded by the anger that there is a vaccine that many people fear or refuse.

Yet, in the face of these complicated feelings, healthcare workers put aside their grief, doing the best they can to ease the next patient's suffering. Hospital primary care doctor Sarah Baron describes continuing to look for "the humanity under the machine, behind the curtain." And when her patient doesn't recover, she is there, helping them transition to death in the most respectful and humane way.

For all of us, the pandemic brings in to stark awareness the reality that death can come for any of us at any moment. And for frontline workers this is true both professionally and personally. Tarah Salazar, a Vanderbilt University nurse, movingly shares the enduring pain she feels at the loss of a loved one from COVID-19.

For Tarah and others, when a traumatic event shatters one's world, especially the death of a loved one, there is a loss of identity, as if a part of the self is missing. Their future, who they thought they would be, will not include this loved one. At first, the mind refuses to accept or integrate the absence of someone essential to oneself, and the incomprehensible event cannot be woven neatly into one's memory. Like a phantom limb, the profound sense of dislocation can be unremitting. There are no words, for this type of pain. The irrevocability of death can make the pain feel unbearable, as if one may not survive.

Research shows that reminiscing and sharing memories are important ways to keep a loved one alive. My own writing began after my daughter died, to give words to my grief and mostly, to keep her with me, to keep her alive on the page, and just maybe, to write me back to life.

To write it is to approach this feeling of grief and loss in real time, with the hope of once again feeling whole and intact, with a future story to tell.

We write to heal ourselves.

A Growing Threat

Anna Wright, MD
Emergency Medicine
Novant Health Kernersville Medical Center
Kernersville, NC

On a February morning in 2020, I walked into the small physicians' charting area in the emergency department. My green backpack made a soft thud as I dropped it on the floor. It was weighty with drinks, snacks, a stethoscope, and the references I needed for my twelve-hour shift.

I saw Dr. Davis[*] sitting in front of the computer. On the screen was a map of the world in which cases of the new virus were depicted as blaring red circles. The size of the circles expanded ominously in step with new infections. Dr. Davis seemed more frazzled than usual as he refreshed the screen for updates.

Navy, wrinkled scrubs hung loosely on his large frame and drooped too low on his hips. His hair was bushy and unbrushed. His beard was wild and unkempt, much like the space where he had spent the last twelve hours working.

The dictation room was littered with Nicorette gum, crumpled paper blood gas results, and piles of EKGs. There were a few cans of diet soda scattered on the counters, and Dr. Davis's bags were haphazardly positioned in the pathway of several rolling chairs.

Over the past year of working with him, I had come to appreciate the warm heart and the medical prowess hiding beneath his chaotic exterior.

---

[*]   His name has been changed to protect his privacy.

This morning as we gazed at the computer, I was looking cautiously at the precipitous cliff of disaster, wondering how bad it would really become. He was already in frantic survival mode preparing for the worst.

I learned the word COVID-19 from him that day. It sounded weird, like a pest or the genus of a newly discovered plant. As the red circles metastasized across the computer-generated map, I had no idea that COVID-19 would reshape the world.

Dr. Davis wanted to take no risks. He walked into patient rooms in a modified scuba mask to supplement the hospital-issued PPE. He stood at the bedsides of patients to ask, "so, what brings you out in a pandemic?" I would have thought the question insensitive if I did not see the stress it contained.

I sat down to take his sign-out, and he rolled his scrub legs up to reveal a red rash all over his legs. He told me about a variety of other physical complaints he had been experiencing. He confessed he had undergone some lab testing during his shift. Maybe he had an autoimmune condition?

His body's creeping red blotches seemed a chillingly ironic nod to the map of COVID-19 cases. He had begun to seem a little more erratic and anxious than usual. Still, he was endearing, and his commitment to his patients and to the practice of medicine remained a larger force than his worry. I thought all the stress was just hitting him hard.

Dr. Davis did not return to work after that month. COVID's initial impact on our hospital resulted in a drastic drop in patient volume, and we no longer needed him as a locum tenens (a temporary traveling) physician. I missed seeing him as the pandemic unfolded, and I wondered how he was holding up during it all.

It was a punch in my stomach when I learned that he had been diagnosed with an advanced brain tumor. He would not be contending with the threat he so feared. A silent, unseen, greater danger lurked inside him instead. His cancer was growing just like the red circles of COVID-19 we had watched that morning.

All this death felt unfair: Elderly nursing-home patients couldn't quarantine from the staff they depended on for their daily care. Immigrant laborers who needed their income from the chicken plants could not avoid standing shoulder to shoulder with other workers. Paramedics who had taken all the right precautions died as vaccines appeared on the horizon.

Dr. Davis was young and dedicated. He had deep knowledge and an outsized heart. He had so much left to give. We started the pandemic journey together, staring down a road we didn't want to imagine. There was so much we didn't know. There were threats we could see and those we couldn't.

Each time I prepared to enter the room of a patient with COVID-19, I reckoned with my own mortality. Would this encounter be the one that infected me? Maybe, I thought as I tied the yellow gown around my neck and slipped purple exam gloves on my hands. With this knowledge, I pushed open the door and took my chances.

Squeezed Dry

Diane Birnbaumer, MD
Emergency Medicine ● Los Angeles, CA

It will be like riding a bicycle. Almost thirty years of experience will undoubtedly bridge the one-year gap between my last ER shift and this one. Right?

The first patient is a gently lobbed softball of a case—not the COVID-19 I expect. A thin, edgy 43-year-old alcoholic, tattoos of tears on his cheek and tombstones on his arms. He was hit by a car last night while riding his bicycle, knocked out when he hit the ground. He came to, got up, and went home. He is here now because his girlfriend wants him to be checked out. So I check him out. He's fine. A couple of quick tests and he's ready to go home. One down. Piece of cake. I breathe more easily.

The overhead speaker crackles. "Purple Team, Critical Medical, Bed 5, ETA 2 minutes." Okay, here we go. In the next moment, the lead paramedic rushes in, clutching the field laptop. He shoves several wrinkled EKGs into my hand. "Chest pain. 39-year-old guy. Looks real."

The EMTs hurriedly roll the gurney into the tiny ER room, and I glance at the patient. I know the look. I've seen it hundreds of times. The bug-eyed, panicked expression. Eyes darting around, sitting bolt upright. Terrified. I hurry to the bedside. In my haste to calm him I forget to put on gloves. I touch his forehead and my hand comes away dripping with his sweat.

His gaze falls full on my face, and then it happens. He says the words. Those words. "I don't want to die. Don't let me die." I draw up short. When a patient says that, they know before we do that death is imminent. Always. And I did it, I said the wrong thing, the words I know never to utter: "We're not going to let you die."

The minute the words are out of my mouth I know it is a promise I cannot keep. He stiffens, becomes board-like, and his arms jerk several times. We don't even have him on the monitor yet, but experience tells me his heart is fibrillating. He's in cardiac arrest. We work on him for almost an hour. His heart stops, starts again. He bucks into the air from the shocks we give, his IV flows with drug after drug, and finally we get his heart started long enough to get him up to the cath lab and into the capable hands of our best cardiologist.

The "Code Blue, Cath Lab" minutes later ends the story. That young man died. I failed him. My second patient after coming back to work in the ER. It isn't that I couldn't save him; no one could. But that I made him a promise I could not keep.

Somewhere out there his family has no idea that the man they kissed goodbye this morning is now gone. I picture them, going about their daily lives, unaware that those lives are now forever changed. For now, I am the keeper of this terrible knowledge.

The ghosts appear: those hundreds of people whose lives have intersected mine in these moments, these life-altering, terrible moments. And I know I just can't absorb any more.

Forever in a Moment

Tarah Salazar
Nurse ● Vanderbilt University
Nashville, Tennessee

The last time I saw you, the moon was shining so bright, a man was playing a rusted guitar in the background, and children were running around our feet, enjoying the warm summer night. Your hair was long, ruffled by the breeze, and your eyes dark, saddened by life's unexpected turns.

The last time I saw you, my heart felt so full, full of hope and excitement for our future.

The last time I saw you your hand fit perfectly in mine, as if each little crease was made specifically for you. The softness of your lips and your smooth skin filled my soul with warmth.

The last time I saw you we planned for our future, together. Your smile brought me comfort and gave me the strength I needed to say our temporary good-bye.

The last time I saw you, I hugged you so tight that for a moment we became one. I cherished your embrace until they made me let go. I did not know that the last time I saw you would be the last time.

Health Care Proxy

Sarah Baron, MD, MS
Montefiore Medical Center
Albert Einstein College of Medicine ❈ Bronx, New York

They have you hooked up to a different kind of ventilator, the kind with the switches and the round dials that turn, analog, sitting like a dictionary on the bedside table. "This is it?" I ask the residents and the respiratory tech, not realizing that you are looking at me. I guess the propofol* (not supposed to be on the floor, but whatever) must not be working. At least the vent is (and is allowed on the floor, also whatever). You look comfortable, but you can mouth words to me, indicate what bothers you. I really want to call your health care proxy—and I ask, "Who is it?" Mouthing an impossible answer, you try three or four times.

Finally, you mime a phone and point to your bag—a small overnight bag for a big woman (I could never fit my stuff in such a small bag). There are some clothes, a toothbrush; in the outside pocket, your wallet and phone—locked. "It's locked," I tell you too loudly, over the wheeze of the machine, but I forget that you can hear despite your other current limitations. You motion for it, with a "come here" hand, barely avoiding the tube, and type in the password (the propofol is definitely not working). You find your sister's name and number and hit call a little prematurely. "Vanessa?" The mouthing of words coalesces: Va - Ne - Ssa. It makes sense now. I tell her, "She has COVID-19, she's on

---

* Propofol is a short-acting medication used for sedation.

a breathing machine, and she is awake. No, you can't visit her. They're taking her to the ICU soon. We'll take good care of her. We'll call you a little later, ok?" This is why I do the work that I do. I got her family on the phone. I know how to listen. I know how to answer, how to search, how to look, how to feel. I found the humanity under the machine, behind the curtain, with your toothbrush, in your bag.

Only later do I realize that the tidal volume is set so high because you can't maintain your oxygenation otherwise. You'll get hurt from those settings, but we don't have a choice. By tomorrow you won't answer any questions, whatever the propofol.

By next week you'll be gone.

Contact

Shobana Ramasamy
Internal Medicine Resident
Vanderbilt Medicine ● Cumming, Georgia

What can be done in six months?
#1. Running through sunlit expanses with loved ones
#2. Re-read your favorite book series
#3. Traveling every checkbox country on your list of dream trips.
Back when the future meant,
After-the-fact
Not the limbo of choicelessness

But, you have less than six months.
Your legs have betrayed you
So running is out of the question.
Your swallow is dysfunctional,
your nutrition arrives through a tube,
And there is
So much
Pain.

The hospital room is dark,
Cold.
White walls, white floor, white sheets.
All the better to see

All that ails,
We hope.

Every person walking in
Trudges in with thin plastic strapped to their bodies
Like flimsy shields,
So unprepared for the unknown.
They,
We,
speak animatedly,
Urgently.
As if begging you,
beseeching your mind
to make swift decisions,
pleading with the disease,
to change course.

When I walked in your room that day
I wanted you to know that I am sorry.
My words haphazardly
Rolled together
How regretful I was.
To not have an answer
To not make this easier
To be wearing this plastic gown,
As if you are dangerous to
Even the cells of my skin.

You grasp my hand.
It is okay.
I will go back to my home,
My country,
To be near those who loved me
From their souls.
And I will be at peace.

Dad

Debra Thompson, Ph.D., LCSW
Private Practice ● Collegeville, Pa.

A search for where you are
Tell me in a dream now
Since you are free and floating
Finally having time for me

Broken
Without boundary or balance
A Ferris wheel ride in reverse
Drenched in the sweat
Of too many choices
You became frozen
And then so did I
The legacy of father to daughter

I tell myself in a dream
I am attending a Broadway play
Lasting all night long
Ending in the morning!
Daylight coming too quickly

You lived in a dangerous city
Without any food, Dad
I look for you still
Over the brightly lit darkness

My Ferris wheel ride moving forward
High and centered
Slowing down without bravado
Hoping for a gentle landing
Grounded
Waiting as the safety bar unlatches
With more help than I need

Purpose

Blaine Robinson
Pediatric Nurse Practitioner
Neonatal Intensive Care Unit ⁕ Nashville, TN

I went into the medical field because I wanted to help others. I wanted to make a difference in people's lives in some way. Over the past eight years working in the Neonatal Intensive Care Unit, I have made countless connections with patients and their families. I have witnessed happy endings where these tiny patients have gone home with their parents, and tragic, sad, unthinkable endings where parents had to say goodbye too soon. My most rewarding moments have been when I was able to connect with a patient and their family whether it was at the beginning of life in the delivery room or at the end of life when providing bereavement care. Compassion throughout end-of-life care can feel like both my purpose and my downfall at times.

It was supposed to be a routine surgery, although nothing about his life thus far had been what someone would consider "normal." He was born with a rare genetic condition that required him to have multiple surgeries. He had healed well from previous procedures, and his parents were some of the most devoted that I have ever encountered in the NICU. They would visit him every day and his mother would climb into his hospital bed with him to comfort him. They were first-time parents, and I connected with them on more of a friend level than I usually allow myself with patient's families. Their kindness and spirituality drew people to them.

The routine surgery turned into this boy's parents' worst nightmare. The baby lost his life in the OR. I was not working that day, but I remember being in my apartment and receiving the phone call that put a terrible pit in my stomach. I was not expecting him to go so soon, and I couldn't imagine how his parents were feeling. They continued to visit the unit and provide donations following his death, and despite their suffering, they focused on helping others. His parents were grateful for the care I gave their son during his life, and although it has now been 6 years since he was here, I still think about him and his family. I think about the love his family showed him and how we tried to make his time on earth as comfortable as we could.

Although I believe connectedness provides purpose in my job, I rarely allow myself to get to that level with my patients. I can feel myself hardening toward families and situations in a form of self-preservation. I have felt the pain of losing patients, and empathizing with families, and I try to resist it, as it has led to burn out. I am still working on finding a successful compromise that allows me to provide the compassionate care that I strive to provide, without allowing it to affect my daily life outside of work.

I believe the human condition requires us to connect with others to live our most fulfilling life.

Betrayal

Debra A. Neumann, Ph.D.
Psychologist and psychoanalyst in private practice
Bethesda, Maryland

Oh moon, crescent moon,

so slight in your abating beauty.

Refracted by my waning vision

into two slivers.

Donning the aura of the rising sun,

You travel with Venus, your companion.

Venus, goddess of love and beauty,

the first morning star.

Or is this a 'False Dmitri' Venus?

A cold, impostor satellite?

Like the ventilator

accompanying you

to your death.

PART IV

Breaking

INTRODUCTION

Kerry L. Malawista, Ph.D.

INCESSANT LOSS, WITH PATIENT AFTER PATIENT DYING, understandably leaves healthcare workers in a state of helplessness. The shortage of staff, the need to fill in extra shifts, exhausts them. With the constant fear of bringing the illness home to loved ones, they remain anxious and on edge. Others are just numb. They suffer with guilt for the lack of compassion they feel for ICU patients who refused vaccinations. Reading and hearing that COVID-19 is a hoax not only angers them but also invalidates their sacrifice. Taken together, the demands of the pandemic have taken a toll on their mental and physical health.

It wasn't until 1980, several years after the end of the Vietnam War, that Post Traumatic Stress Disorder (PTSD) was included in the DSM-III and recognized as a psychological illness. No longer a short-term response to a traumatic situation, PTSD is defined as an enduring disease that may affect anyone who has lived through a horrifying situation.

Frederic Dutheil (2020)[1] and other researchers in France found that the COVID-19 pandemic is classifiable as a traumatic event of exceptional magnitude. With its ongoing exposure and risk of death, the pandemic transcends the range of normal human experience. A body under stress, whether soldiers, children living in violent environments or frontline workers, wreaks havoc not only on the mind, but can damage the body: Blood pressure rises, the immune system weakens, and the heart muscle permanently damaged.

Yet, acute trauma doesn't always lead to acute suffering; not all healthcare workers that are stressed and burned out have PTSD. For many who work in emergency rooms, go to war, or lose a loved one suffer acutely, resilience slowly returns.

Researchers have shown that writing about loss and traumatic experiences have health benefits, including strengthening the immune system. In a 2006 study by Kin-Ming Chan and Karen Horneffer[2] asked young adults to spend 15 minutes, twice a week, journaling or drawing about a stressful event, or writing about their plans for the day. Those who journaled had a reduction in such symptoms as depression, anxiety, and hostility.

Let's imagine we are Sarah Edward, hearing her patient shout, "I can't breathe! I can't breathe!" Her words an echo of George Floyd as he was choked to death and all that was—and is— happening in the world. Whatever decision Sarah makes next can mean life or death for this young woman. The haunting image of her patient will likely remain with Sarah for months and years to come. As we saw with George Floyd, when we witness another's suffering, we experience the nearly unavoidable domino effect of secondary trauma, also known as vicarious traumatization.

When memories are too overwhelming to write about, we can protect our self by using metaphors or by fictionalizing the account. Tim O'Brien's novel, *The Things They Carried*, whose work this project is named for, creates metaphors to describe a brutal death. When the character Ted Lavender is shot and killed, O'Brien writes, "Kiowa, who saw it happen, said it was like watching a rock fall, or a big sandbag or something–just boom, then down–not like the movies where the dead guy rolls around and does fancy spins…"

Savannah Willingham, a hospice worker, shares a dream of holding a dying baby, and wakes "carrying the grief of someone else's story, my eyes still tinged red and a warm weight on my chest."

Yet it is often in moments of calm, when life slows, that the feelings hit. Margaret Tehven writes of working in the ICU, the constant questioning, "How many people will we fail?" But it is not until she leaves work and sees a shivering baby rabbit that all the feelings hit her. She thinks, "I have to help it

---

2   Chan, K.M., & K. Horneffer. 2006. Emotional expression and psychological symptoms: A comparison of writing and drawing. The Arts in Psychotherapy, 33(1), 26-36

but I don't know how." She panics that she will make the wrong decision and the rabbit will die. "I finally gently nudge it under a nearby bush and hope it stays sheltered. I hope. I hope. I reach my car and realize I'm crying. This is the first time I've cried in months."

In our writing workshops, participants spoke and wrote about the stress of having to choose which patients should receive ventilators, in essence, deciding who will live or who will die. The extraordinary demand on healthcare workers leave them battered by memories and flashbacks, continually reliving the past in the present.

While we know more than we did at the start of the pandemic, there remain many unknowns of what lies ahead. As a country we need to recognize the many overworked health care workers who under the stress of exhaustion are no longer able to do their job well or who are spent. Many have left medicine, like participant Molly Phelps, an ER doctor for 18 years who touchingly wrote me.

Dear Dr. Malawista,

We have never met, but you have undoubtedly changed the course of my life. I am an ER doctor in California and was on my way to get groceries on a random Wednesday this summer when your NPR piece with Dr. Schmitz came on and I unexpectedly found myself viscerally sobbing. I had to pull my car over as my body heaved and an unappealing mixture of saliva, snot, and tears fell in fat drops on the console. Ironically, I was out of Kleenex and had to use an old surgical mask as a tissue.

I signed up for a Things They Carry Project workshop with Ruth Neubauer and Sally Steenland and remember their looks of empathy, and at times horror and perhaps pity when I shared my writing. It was clear that what was "no big deal" to me because it was "not nearly as bad as NY and India" was actually still pretty intense and not at all normal in the real world. Their kindness and sensitivity held up a mirror for me to look at my rather traumatic pandemic experiences more objectively and start to process and grieve.

Unbeknownst to me, the writing prompts from the project you created ended up cracking open the secret box I had nailed shut and pushed down as far as it would go. It was on another random Wednesday, two days after my final workshop, that the box blew open and a quiet, peaceful, matter-of-fact statement made itself known. "I am done. I have given enough and it is okay for me to walk away and be happy again."

Leaving medicine was something I had literally never consciously thought about before, but it was also exactly right. I resigned and worked my last shift two weeks ago. I don't know how my next chapter will unfold, but I am certain it will be with more hope and happiness thanks to you.

Warmly, Molly

At times, strong feelings and memories, may be too overwhelming to continually re-live. Molly may have intuited that repeatedly returning to the same setting she runs the risk of making trauma ruts in her memory. Since memory is easily distorted, there is the risk of amplifying the trauma, rather than decreasing the images. In these situations, it is better to let the scar heal over and not continuously pick at the scab.

Strength may come in finding ways to keep going. As Molly Phelps shared, strength may mean knowing when it is time to stop.

I CAN'T BREATHE

Sarah Edwards, RN
ER ✹ St. Francis Medical Center
Lynwood, California

I've taken care of her for hours. Young. 28. Kidneys shot by lupus. Fluid overload. She needs dialysis and my 20 bed ER can't…won't do it. It would have to wait until she got her bed. I ask her "What do you like to do when you're not sick?" She tells me how she loves taking care of her little sister. I smile. We wait for her bed. It never comes. She's on a bed pan. She's yelling my name in fear.

"I can't breathe! I can't breathe!" she calls.

I tell the doctor we don't have a good line. Why don't we have a better line? He tries a central line as she gasps for breath.

She's drowning.

Drowning on her own lungs. She's seizing.

Alarms ring.

"Bag her!" the doctor yells at me. The bag is the wrong size. Why didn't I check? It's my fault, it's all my fault. Nurses run in. Someone throws another bag at me. I catch it like a football and then squeeze air into her lungs.

Crash carts, tubes, orders, chaos.

She comes to and screams. My ears and the halls ring with a guttural, visceral cry. Her parents hear. They are still and silent; sad and helpless. What did I miss? How did this happen? She's tubed and stabilized but barely. Bilevel vent. The hail-mary of vent settings.

She's fighting the vent.

Alarms never stop. She's whisked to ICU with a team of nurses. I call the ICU. I'm put on hold.

"You don't understand," I'm yelling, "This patient is coming now."

Did she make it? Is she okay?

I'm spiraling.

I can't breathe. I can't breathe.

Sugar in My Coffee

Savannah Willingham
Hospice CAN II/ Certified End of Life Doula
Asheville, North Carolina

Some mornings I put extra sugar in my coffee.

Like the morning I woke from the dream of the death of a son I never had. In the dream that created him, I watched his birth, knowing he was already dying. I held his tiny form in a warm bath against my naked body because it was the only thing that gave him comfort from all the medical tubes and inflamed skin. I could feel the feverish tint of his small torso, and the weight of his whole life leaking out with every gasping breath.

So, I held him close and imagined a life for him. Of growing so much taller than me that he would laugh about it when he reached for things over my head. Of the rough scrape of his well-groomed beard when he kissed my cheek goodbye after holiday dinners.

I gave him heartbreak from those who weren't good enough for him, but only enough to let him learn what real love feels like, so he'd never want to let it go.

And I didn't let it go.

That tiny boy whose whole life I gave to him in between counted dying breaths. That I held against my chest until I could feel the indention of his emptying soul in my heart. Till I woke. In my bed.

My face tickling with hot tears that spilled across my cheeks, even as I remembered that I never had a son.

So I got up, carrying the grief of someone else's story, my eyes still tinged red and a warm weight on my chest.

And I put some extra sugar in my coffee.

Rabbit

Margaret Tehven, RN
ICU at Abbot Northwestern Hospital
Minneapolis, Minnesota

We get three admits in a row; all young, all Hispanic, all from southern Minnesota, and all very sick. It's early May 2020, and Minnesota is experiencing its first COVID-19 surge. We open another set of beds to accommodate the admits. Nurses, doctors, aids, and respiratory techs rush to pull in more beds, stock the rooms, prep the intubation equipment, push ventilators, and line carts into place. The three patients are quickly intubated and one of them is paralyzed and prone. I wonder if they caught the virus at work, or at home. I'm angry—maybe they had no choice but to go to work or were given little choice on how to protect themselves and their family. What kind of employer does that during a pandemic?

I'm circulating in the Intensive Care Unit (ICU) tonight, where trouble is brewing and extra hands are needed. Adrenaline is buzzing through the unit. We all wonder, "Is this it? Will it be like New York or Italy? How many people will we fail?" Alarms and monitors ring and beep loudly as a doctor leads us through a difficult intubation. I have been running all shift, and sweat condenses under my N95 mask, making my face feel wet and sticky. The mask dulls the smells from the unit, but the vinegary chemical scent of the mask prickles my nostrils, even though this is my third shift wearing it. Two more shifts and I'll get a new one.

This shift is rough, we're doing everything we can, but have no idea if any of these patients will make it through. At midnight, I leave the hospital. The air is near freezing, and I can see my breath in the drizzle. I make my way across the street to the parking lot, tired and drained. I look up as I step off the curb and see a baby rabbit shivering on the sidewalk. I'm pinned to the ground; I just stare at it. I have to help it but I don't know how. If I touch it, will its mother reject it? If I leave it, will it make it through the night? It feels like I stand there for hours, staring at the rabbit as it trembles and tries to make itself smaller. I finally gently nudge it under a nearby bush and hope it stays sheltered. I hope. I hope. I reach my car and realize I'm crying. This is the first time I've cried in months.

I find I am not alone in this; I tell my coworker about the rabbit. He nods and says," It was the Christmas dishes for me I dropped a box of them moving and just broke down." Another nurse adds, "I cried over burnt chocolate chip cookies, and I don't even like chocolate chip cookies."

Meditate on This

Amelia Sauter, LSCW
Psychotherapist Trumansburg, NY

Every. Fucking. Day. That's how often I meditated during the first year of the pandemic. And for what? They say it quiets the mind, but that is an outright lie. Or at least not exactly true—maybe simply a misstatement, or a sly understatement. Sure, meditation has potential: you sit down, you settle in, you pay attention to your breath, and then WHAM there it all is: Everything you absolutely do not want to notice, all the garbage you don't want to feel.

They don't call it garbage. They call it thoughts, feelings, body sensations. I call it turds. Big, fat turds. Bring compassion to all of it, they say. Compassion for garbage? Compassion for turds? That's the suggestion? Here's what that would look like: big, fat compassion-frosted turds.

Meditation sounds so peaceful, doesn't it? Don't buy it! You will be meditating with turds! It's stinky, it's messy, and when you look into the bowels that the turds burst forth from, there is a war between the shoulds and the have-tos and the what-ifs. Like an existential unresolvable irritable bowel syndrome. I'm supposed meditate on that?

The first email during the pandemic I got from a teen's parent—and all the parent emails after it—went like this: "My child won't get out of bed in the morning. They aren't signing into their online classes. They aren't showering and won't come out of their rooms except for meals, and when they do, they hardly eat. Tell us what to do, Amelia! You're the therapist—help us! Fix our child, tell us how to survive this soul-crushing nightmare!"

I start to write back, "I have no fucking idea. I've never done this before." I delete the first line and begin again. "I wish I had answers. We are all in this together, and we're going to have to figure it out together."

And so, I meditate with turds: the turd of not knowing. The turd of new responsibilities I didn't sign up for. The turd of failure. I want meditation to relieve me of the turds, and the suffering it causes. I want a moment of peace. I want to feel like I did the summer I was twelve when my visiting cousin got so annoying that I quietly escaped to my room and slid under my bed.

The polished hardwood floor under there was stone cold, even in July. There was no dust; my mother obsessively saw to that. I felt my eyes adjust to the darkness. As I stared up at the bedsprings that I could only vaguely make out, I exhaled. I hadn't even realized I was holding my breath.

There is something about the absence of everything: No light. No warmth. No people. Nothing to do. Nothing to react to. I could hear the muffled voices downstairs, but they felt far away, and I felt protected by something. I heard my cousin ask my mother where I was. "I'm sure she'll be back," my mother said, "when she's ready." Somehow, she knew. I felt understood.

This is how I want to feel now when I meditate. I want to be held by the darkness. I want to feel nothing, the absence of everything. But instead, I am greeted by loud, obnoxious turds.

How do I know I'm a good therapist? What if I'm just making things up? Yes, I listen, I validate, I ask thoughtful questions, and I genuinely care. And I also make shit up. I've never done this pandemic thing before. Have you? Have any of us? What do I know? What if I'm fooling everyone, and I actually don't know anything at all?

When I sit down to meditate, and I reach the point where I can't stand sitting with my turds one more fucking minute, I practice a type of meditation called Tonglen. You inhale and acknowledge your own struggle, your turds, and as you exhale you hold them in your heart. Yuk and gross and why the hell would I want to do that? And on the next breath, you inhale the pain and suffering of all the millions of people in the world who feel the same way that you do right now, in this very moment, and then you exhale and your heart expands to hold all of them, and it fills with compassion and you say,

Ohhhhh. This is why I meditate.

I Am You

Denise Montagnino, DO, MPH
OB/GYN ◦ Nashville, Tennessee

Jump in,
Jump in and introduce yourself.
My name's Denise
Yeah
And I'm from Boca
Yeah
And I'm a Gator
Yeah
All right
All right
All right

Hi!
My name is Denise and I am an addict. I have a work addiction.
Hi!
My name is Denise and I have a shame problem.
Hi!
My name is Denise and I don't know what else to say.

Who am I?

I am
Mother Wife Doctor Daughter Sister
I am
a child
I am
an adult
I am
an obstetrician gynecologist

You mean who/what is my identity
You don't want to know who I am
I am lost
I am seeking I am praying I am finding
I am walking I am running I am crying
I am fighting

For what you ask
For my identity back
I want it back
You stole it from me
Now it is time to seek it out
Get it back
Truth
Whole truth

So what is my truth
You want to know
Of course you do
You want my secrets
My brokenness
My sorrow
My suffering

So there
There it is
I will lay it all down
All out for you to see

Now do you still love me?
Am I still yours?
Do you want me to take it all back?
Well I cannot

It's too late

Endings and Beginnings

Rachel Kadar, MD
Intensive Care Unit Physician ⚬ Chicago, Illinois

July 13th, 2021—the day that finally, for the first time in 15 months, I took care of <u>zero</u> COVID patients. The first day when life almost seemed normal. The first day I hesitated as I completed my daily decontamination ritual at the front door, thinking, do I really need this anymore? Can I actually hug my kids before running straight to the shower? Vaccines: the savior of the pandemic.

But I am not so optimistic that this is really the end. Unfortunately, many people are rejecting the savior. They are refusing to listen to what will free them from suffering and death. One hospital system in Missouri has higher COVID hospitalizations and deaths now than at the height of the pandemic in January. They are drowning with COVID patients, sometimes transferring them to outside facilities because they are out of beds. How many have the shield of vaccination there? Not enough, not enough to fight the war.

As I read the news I start to wonder, how many are vaccinated here? When Delta comes through will it be like in Missouri? Will I once again be thrust into an overflowing COVID ICU, full of sick and dying patients on life support fighting for their lives? Will I once again have to run around the hospital intubating the patients who look like they are drowning in their own secretions, struggling to breathe, asking them to call their families before I intubate them, because it may be the last time they ever speak to them? Will I have to watch the fear in their eyes when I tell them that they will die if I don't place them on life support? Even then, I cannot guarantee they will live.

Can I really do it again? Thoughts race through my head. Will I break? Will I scream at all of the unvaccinated, telling them they did this to themselves? No. No, I won't scream, I won't break. I CAN do it again. I will continue to work tirelessly to save the lives of those who are unvaccinated—those who choose to live their lives while putting others at risk. Do I treat the drunk driver any differently as a patient even when he has killed my patient next door? What about the drug addict? No, they are all people, and they are all my patients. I am a soldier, fighting a war; a war against COVID, a war against disease.

The general population gets to choose if they want to end the war. They can all get vaccinated and the war will end. They have a choice. But unfortunately, I DON'T have a choice: other people's "freedom" to make uneducated choices sends me back to war— back to the hell that is the COVID ICU.

July 17th, July 18th, no COVID patients still. I ask one of my patients in the ICU, who is not here with COVID, if she's been vaccinated. "No," she says. I educate her on the benefits of vaccination, remind her that Delta is coming, and request that she get vaccinated. She listens but it's unclear if she will follow through. As I walk out of the room, I hold my breath, I say a prayer. If others spent one day in my shoes, they would be lining up to get vaccinated, just like all my colleagues. Lucky for them, they don't see my world. Or maybe it's unlucky for them, because if they did see my COVID ICU, they would have the same vaccination shield that I do. If they saw my world, they would see vaccines as the true savior they really are.

July 21st, a COVID ICU admission. July 22nd, I admit two more. By August, one third of the intensive care unit consists of COVID patients, on ventilators, fighting for their lives. Another 50 COVID patients sit on the hospital floors requiring oxygen, their fate to be determined. All unvaccinated. This is unfortunately all too familiar. The next surge is here. I just pray it's mild; I pray I don't break; I pray it ends soon.

Animal Crackers

Craig R Sussman, MD
Associate Professor of Clinical Medicine
Vanderbilt University Medical Center ⊛ Nashville, Tennessee

I am angry! I am sad! I am frustrated! I have had enough of this!

When COVID appeared 18 months ago, most of us medical people decided to approach it as a battle for which we had spent our careers preparing. After all, I was Chief Resident at Temple University Hospital on July 2, 1976, when the Legionnaire's Convention created a "terrible" pandemic. I remember how we handled it. We organized, planned, and worked together to defeat it. Within 1 month, we had succeeded.

When COVID struck, it was deja vu. I was enthusiastic about jumping in and planning our strategy. After all, we had mastered it the last time.

I am fortunate to know several people who are world experts in COVID viruses and vaccines. These are clinicians and researchers who have been at the forefront of infectious diseases.

I researched the latest data every day and took my place as a primary care physician. Since this virus was so new and so dangerous, we had to unite, mobilize, and anticipate. Yes, every recommendation had to be a hypothesis, an educated guess.

Where did the disease come from? Who was vulnerable? How can we protect ourselves?
How can we protect our patients, friends, family? What can we do in our communities?

The two spokesmen and experts that I trust and follow, Dr. Anthony Fauci and Dr. Bill Schaffner spoke every day on the news. I was so amazed by their calm, direct, and deliberate approach. My colleagues at Vanderbilt digested and summarized the data every day.

We clinicians organized and planned. I was amazed by the accuracy of so many of the guesses. Sure, you can't bet on your recommendations, but with the infinite number of questions, they were amazingly on target. We fought, we succeeded, we failed, we counseled, we cried. We worried about our families, coworkers, patients, and ourselves. We researched it and listened carefully so that we could advise accurately.

Did we succeed? I truly believe that this would have been an 18- to 24-month battle that would relent.

Where are we now? I watched in horror recently as many of my colleagues participated in a suburban county school board meeting. The experts calmly discussed the recommendations for wearing masks, social distancing, and vaccination. The hate and hostility that the community expressed to them! And the threats, "We know where you live and we will come after you."

Why are people not listening and not getting vaccinated? How can people who have depended on me for over 35 years not respect my advice? Who are they listening to that has more credibility? I have tried.

I am now on an inpatient hospital service. There are over 130 patients with COVID, and several are on respirators. Over 90 percent of these patients were not vaccinated, by their own choice.

Every day we are working long hours trying to get our overwhelming work done.

The other afternoon, I must have appeared down and stressed sitting in an ICU. A nurse threw a package of animal crackers in my lap. I looked up, startled and said, "I have genuinely tried every coping mechanism that I know of: focus on something positive, get sleep, exercise, do yoga. . . ."

The nurse turned to me with a smile, "Yes, but have you tried animal crackers?"

I stopped, looked up, devoured them, and smiled. "You gave me a moment of delight. You made my day. Thank you."

Screens That Divide Us

Karen Dybner-Madero, Psy.D
Consultant to Delaware County Office of Children and Youth Services
Delaware County ◦ Private Practice ◦ Philadelphia, PA

I sit across from her. I sit across from him. I sit across from them. The screen is our divide. Or maybe the screen just pretends this is all that divides us. But in actuality, it goes so much further than that. I know this, somewhere deep inside.

They are trying, most of them anyway, to comply with my requests to share information about themselves. Even with this new virtual world we need to live in, I know they are trying. I listen to them, and believe that almost all of them, in some way or another, do care. Really. They want to be the best mom, the best dad, the best child. But their lives, not all of them, but so many of them, are really hard. So damn hard.

I used to think about this when I was younger—a realization that some kids just had it worse than I did. Their parents were too strict, they got yelled at, they got beaten. I used to wonder why was I so lucky to have the parents I got? And to this day, when I hear about how someone has to relive the trauma of being beaten or touched, for no reason—except that once they were innocent and living in a house where another person knew they could do this to them— it makes me want to cry too. I look and see how the woman who is trying hard to keep it together, begins to shake and her tears well up, and she is almost moaning in pain that she has tried to push back. Her face takes up the whole screen, and I want to offer her the tissue I have next to me. But of course, that won't do today. Our screen divides us.

She has eight kids, she is not yet 40, and she has just completed her time in a halfway house. She wants to get all her kids back, she tells me. All of them are with relatives, except her youngest, the one she delivered in jail. He is with her best friend from childhood. He has been raised by this friend, who has now turned against her and wants to "keep him." I ask her if she's thought about how her son may feel having to leave the only home he has known. She admits that this may be hard, but "after all, I'm his mom. He needs to know that he is loved by his family."

On another day, I will have to meet with her on one screen and her son on another, and then this boy and his foster mom. I will have to provide a recommendation for the court, about where I think he should live. My gut tells me, that of course, he needs to stay where he is. He is loved and protected and cared for in a way that is healthy for him. There is no doubt that he has a secure attachment to this foster mother and family. They are his emotional family. But the sadness in his mom's eyes, the one I see on the screen, all she has lived through, things she didn't ask for. And now trying to re-establish a relationship with a son she doesn't know through virtual meetings. My stomach tightens up. I know I am adding to her list of people who have hurt her. I try to rationalize this, to keep in mind what is in the best interest of the child. But I can't.

When I used to wonder why some people had it worse than me, I didn't think I would also be playing a role in all this. I hate my job. I hate myself. I hate this screen.

Salt Water Wounds

Tarah Salazar
Nurse ◉ Vanderbilt University
Nashville, Tennessee

Looking out beyond the hills, past the winding roads and passing cars, past the children building castles, and parents lounging in folding chairs soaking up the sun, through all of the noise and the tears from her bloodshot eyes, she felt an overwhelming calm. She hyper-focused on the waves as they continued to crash, facing rejection from the shore, but nonetheless persisting, fighting on, begging to be loved by a predisposed companion. The weight of the unspoken truth, and the bandages unable to stop the bleeding, brought her to her knees, begging for the strength to stop the tears, to stop her soul from aching, to stop the emotional hemorrhage and grief-stricken pain. She begged and pleaded, outward toward the vast sea breeze, desperate for a cure to her ailment, to mend her bruised and broken armor, and yet the waves continued on, crashing, breaking, and receding.

The roar of the ocean called to her like a siren calling to lonely sailors, entrancing her, craving her existence, inviting her to sit and examine the mystical way of the ocean. As she inched closer, the voices of her family and friends reminding her to be strong, to be brave, not to let this break her began to fade as the ocean's melody grew louder, reminding her to simply be.

The water crept toward her, slow, calm, almost as if waiting for a personal invitation. The salt seeped into her wounds, burning her raw open flesh, inflicting pain at the surface and simultaneously soothing her heartache. The water surrounded her and comforted her beaten and wounded body. Her wounds were hers forever, to mend and heal and eventually scar, but in that moment, as she became intertwined with the ocean, she realized that she had no control over the wounds that would claim her, but instead, only what she would allow to fill their open spaces.

PART V

Finding Hope

INTRODUCTION

Kerry L. Malawista, Ph.D.

TO NOT BE BROKEN, STRESSED, OR BURNED-OUT BY exhaustion, hope is essential. The hospitalist Jennifer Caputo-Seidler describes five recent COVID-19 cases as triumphant, "[I]t doesn't feel like the same crushing wave of having every bed in the ICU full. There is time to breathe, to process the weight of what is happening to each of these patients. This feels like hope."

The risk for healthcare workers, like all of us, is that each time we see a glimmer of possibility or think we have turned a corner, a new variant appears. Then, as was happening at the end of 2021, when a new variant like Omicron arrives we lose hope, we risk isolating ourselves from others and think why bother, all my hard work is pointless. It's a demoralized, lonely place.

Elizabeth Mitchell, an emergency room physician, movingly describes the cycle of hope, followed by a surge of cases, and hope being abandoned.

Elizabeth Armstrong, a primary care physician, tells of returning for a refresher course in advanced cardiovascular life support (ACLS). She experiences this two-year re-credentialing ritual as "an act of hope to practice resuscitation, even though I know for most people whose hearts stop beating, it will be the end of their life, no matter how high quality the CPR, and how rapidly they get defibrillated. Dead is often just dead. But sometimes we can make a difference and give someone a second chance to live their life."

Healthcare workers need to continually find ways to refresh, find meaning in their work, so that they can put their scrubs back on and return to the work they love.

Five Full Beds

Jennifer Caputo-Seidler, MD
Hospitalist • Tampa, Florida

I am back in the COVID ICU, but this week is different. I joke that I am not earning my paycheck this week because we only have 5 COVID patients. It somehow feels triumphant even though each case is still devastating.

There's the retired physician from our hospital. Most of the team doesn't remember her, but I've been here long enough that she and I shared patients when I was a resident. Unfortunately, it doesn't look like she is going to survive. Years of substance use have estranged her from her family. It's heartbreaking to see a former colleague in this position.

There's the army veteran who met his wife on a tour of duty. They've been married 20 years, and she calls him her rock. He's been with us long enough that he is no longer contagious, so I stand beside his wife as she holds his hand and thanks me for the daily phone calls that have sustained her through this ordeal.

There's the middle-aged man that was on intubation watch for days. He had us worried, but now he's recovering. He'll go home later this week. He's one of our successes.

There's the family patriarch who wouldn't wake up when we stopped his sedation. The MRI showed a massive stroke. His family decided on comfort measures, knowing he would not want to live in a facility attached to a trach and ventilator. He was surrounded by his family when we extubated him. I'm grateful it was their hands holding his as he died, even though it reminds me of all those who died without their families.

There's the man brought in by a family member on the brink of death. I didn't think he would make it through that first day, and I tried to prepare his family for that. Miraculously we were able to stabilize him, and by the second day, we were even talking about getting him off the ventilator.

Each patient is still suffering immensely, and each phone call to their families to discuss their critical state and the possibility that they may not survive is gutting. Still, it doesn't feel like the same crushing wave of having every bed in the ICU full. There is time to breathe, to process the weight of what is happening to each of these patients. This feels like hope.

Skills Update

Elizabeth Armstrong, MD
Primary Care Physician
Northampton, Massachusetts

I spent yesterday, September 11, refreshing my advanced cardiovascular life support (ACLS) credentials, as I have done every two years since 2001. It has a ritual feeling to it, coming together with colleagues whom I haven't seen in months; drinking stale coffee out of the vending machine in the training room with the stained, slightly musty carpet, watching hours of over-acted educational videos, and reviewing protocols on laminated cards.

We gather anxiously around the table where an armless, legless plastic mannequin lies, and pretend they are a live human being whom we can save from dying with the right combination of chest compressions, medications, and electric shocks. And then we pretend they have died again, and once again we bring them back. It's play-acting, but it's also practice for real life, like kids playing in a toy kitchen practicing to make dinner.

I usually love it; it feels like an act of hope to practice resuscitation, even though I know for most people whose hearts stop beating, it will be the end of their life, no matter how high quality the CPR, and how rapidly they get defibrillated. Dead is often just dead. But sometimes we can make a difference and give someone a second chance to live their life.

But yesterday I felt sad and unsettled, to be practicing my ACLS skills on the 20th anniversary of 9/11, when almost 3,000 people were killed in ways that ACLS could not help them, and in the middle of a pandemic, when

ACLS seems less relevant. What's the point of restarting someone's heart in my outpatient office, if the hospital I send them to is on diversion and has no ICU beds? It feels a little ludicrous to act as though heart disease is the biggest threat to my patients this year, when it is the virus that killed almost all of the patients I've lost in the past 18 months.

I keep my ACLS skills active as an act of hope. I pray that they will one day feel more relevant again.

charting course

Elizabeth Mitchell, MD
Department of Emergency Medicine
Boston, Massachusetts

I watch the charts
curves heading up
surges now so many
I have lost count.

I remember the summer
we felt freed. we thought it was over.
we tore masks from our faces
after the cases stopped coming
crashing into our doors.
But it wasn't gone and we weren't safe
and it returned as the leaves changed
only this time it was an unwelcome relative
knocking at the window.

We weren't scared
we were tired, and irritable, and losing hope
until
the vaccine arrived at Christmas and we were
ecstatic, overjoyed, jubilant, filled with
indescribable relief.

and so many were saved.
and so many didn't listen, didn't know, didn't understand
our grief and anger and fear and vulnerability
and now they are dying and once again
we watch the charts
as seasons change
the upward curve
the surge that
never ends

Leaving without Limping

Deborah Bernstein, MD
Physician ◦ Homeless residence
Brooklyn, NY

She came into the exam room walking with a rollator, shuffling her swollen red feet and lower legs, limping with pain, overweight, disheveled, and scared. She had been living on the street for ten years, frostbite necessitating toe amputations. When she had no more fight in her, she was dragged to the hospital and rehab and is now well and living at the houseless-homeless shelter.

We start with repairing her hip; she had picked out her doctor and done her research—ever organized, intelligent, and sensible. Her recovery is swift and uneventful.

Then COVID hit and the women from the houseless-homeless shelter were relegated to a motel in East New York, the armpit of Brooklyn, where it is dangerous and frightening; where people shoot up on the sidewalk, and then fall down. Over several weeks, she organized and helped get the women moved to a midtown hotel.

"It is a new year, and she comes back, this feisty Irish lady. I come back too, now vaccinated." Her long wish list is made down to electrolysis of her facial hair. We have long, social appointments during which she tells me about her surgeon brother and swimming in ponds in Massachusetts. She texts me Mother's Day greetings as well as a request for med refills. Her health maintenance and screening are done, and she is eager to be well. She runs toward the liberation, and contradictorily, the weight of personal responsibility.

She still walks with a rollator, much faster now, with no limp, bright of countenance. She describes the view from her SRO (single room occupancy) over the Hudson River as the best she has ever had, the sun sets and rises, the colors of the sky, the trees on Broadway.

And three months later, where is she? She won't answer my phone calls or my attempts to go to her apartment. She lives in her SRO and would view a visit as an interference or infringement.

She is vaccinated for whatever her future holds.

Your Hand

Danielle H. Maxonight, LCSW
Attachment-based therapist for parents and children
Asheville, NC

When I look at your hand, splashed and splotted with bright watercolors, I remember playing handclap games, in the time before. I remember swatting a balloon back and forth, it sometimes hitting a nose or an elbow or a lamp and laughing with surprise. I remember when we could join hands, and eyes, and minds, and hearts, and hope washes over me. I look at your handwriting, now that you're eleven (not nine), and I see how grown-up and how not-yet-grown-up you are: "Thanks for doing this fun thing with me. I think my mom liked it too."

Feeling the crinkles and creases in the paper with my own fingers, I know that you touched this with your little hands too. And somehow, I know that my hand is up on your wall. Or buried in your room, covered with half-read books of all topics, that your mom said are parted with all manner of "bookmarks"–socks, action figures, other books.

I wonder how big your hands will be when I can give you the high five and hug you so badly deserve. I wonder if our wave goodbye over the screen was the real and forever goodbye. I wonder when you'll be able to play Dungeons and Dragons with your new friends, the friends you'd been looking for your whole life. I wonder when your mom will sleep again, when you'll take your mask off at school, or if you've gotten to hug your grandma yet. I have a box full of handprints, but yours is on my wall, because I wonder and I hope and I wait, and I need to wonder and hope and wait.

We waved goodbye, but I guess I'm not ready to let go of the wondering, hoping, and waiting.

What Matters

Sarah A., MD

Infectious Disease Physician • New York City

Much of my work feels thankless. I treat patients with chronic tracheostomies on mechanical ventilation; and those with sacral decubitus ulcers that emit a smell permeating the entire patient hallway (now concealed by our masks). I treat patients who are "growing a garden" of bacteria that has entered their bloodstream, and others for whom a long course of antibiotics will make no difference, only prolong their pain and agony and increase the likelihood of future antibiotic-resistant bacteria.

However, there is so much I am thankful for. To sit with a patient, to listen, and not run away to the next task. To be there when you know that a patient's world is changing and that their life will never be the same. That the woman, only 33 years old, with COVID cardiomyopathy in the cardiac care unit on hemodynamic support, smiles because she saw your face. That I held the frail hand of a woman in COVID isolation, and on several liters of oxygen, when visitors were not allowed to see her, and nurses entered her room less frequently. Even when I can offer no treatment, I know that it matters that I am there, and for that I am thankful.

Punch Doll

Dipanwita Saha, MD, FAAP
Regional Champion for Quality and Safety
PM Pediatrics ◉ Columbia, Maryland

Prior to getting COVID and even while going through divorce from the man I have loved the most in my life, I used imagery to get through tough, heart-wrenching life experiences. Get punched and get back up again and do it over and over and over. Like a punch doll: Light, flexible, and springy.

But after being a doctor during a pandemic and having COVID myself, that spring malfunctioned. The air got let out of the imagery and from my resilience. The punch doll transformed into something heavy, like a rock. I kept falling into the abyss and kept grabbing at things to slow the fall or hold on from falling further down, but nothing worked. When I finally stopped falling, I could see how far down into the dark I was.

At first, I just lay there, flat and unable to even stand. When I tried to climb up the walls into the light, my knees hurt, my chest hurt, my soul and spirit hurt. But I never did give up.

Today, months later, I am nowhere near where I was, but I feel hopeful that I can fill my mind and spirit with resilience again. To be like a punch doll again.

The Weight

Michael Schmitz, DO
Emergency Medicine ● Biddeford, Maine

The practice of medicine contains its own "middle distance"—a territory without discrete boundaries where the foreground, dominated by science, segues into a horizon governed by philosophy and ethics. The practice of medicine relies on comprehension of a hidden curriculum: the ongoing challenge to maintain perspective while witnessing what Nature allows and science helps us understand, with what we believe to be morally just. As an ER physician and former paramedic, my most challenging experiences came from witnessing those competing forces shape the outcome of another person's life.

Physicians often use the term "the art of medicine" to describe what painters refer to as the "middle distance," which I can assure you is not an accidental term. In my experience, the image created with this perspective is endlessly fascinating, at times bittersweet, but most of all, it is breathtaking. Medical education also emphasizes the importance of 3-d perspective, but in a more barbaric and grueling format: organic chemistry.

Organic chemistry (a.k.a "Orgo") is the bane of every pre-med student's existence. It's the weed-out class and, perhaps, the single most crucial grade on your undergraduate transcript. Comprehension of the subject matter relies on recalling a large volume of information and comparing different molecules based on rules used to describe and classify them relative to their three-dimensional structure. The latter is essential because, in some cases, two molecules can be comprised of identical numbers of elements and be oriented around the same atom (its chiral center) but be mirror images of one another instead of identical. Each rotates light differently, and each molecule is distinct. A pair of molecules demonstrating this relationship are called enantiomers. A demonstrable example of this relationship is your left with your right hand. Absent scars or surgical defects, most people's hands are identical in terms of the direction and position of bones, tendons, nerves, and major blood vessels. While facing palm-to-palm, they are mirror images. When compared with both facing downward, they are not identical. (Which is why right and left-handed gloves are necessary.)

Enantiomers illustrate the ability of perspective to create a more profound meaning from difficult experiences. Start by imagining matching events as the "chiral center" of two separate molecules, each with a fixed, standard mass comprising the same components. The elegance of Nature's design reminds us that the event itself, or the weight of the molecule, cannot be changed; how the final product interacts with the environment is however in our control. The Stoics address this point by reminding us to view challenges as obstacles and posit that we empower ourselves to derive meaning by first accepting our inability to change an event.

At a patient's bedside, I find that this perspective permits separation of the unavoidable anguish or emotional pain of bearing witness to difficult experiences—the "I was there, I saw it happen, we did what we could, and damn, this really hurts"—from our conclusions. We must carry the experience forward. For me, describing the event as weight is a choice that empowers me to derive meaning from it. I believe the product, in this example, is either an experience of suffering or of empathy. While these two words are not, by definition, antonyms, describing them as enantiomers bolsters resilience without denying the associated emotions or feelings.

But my chemical analogy does not address the effect of the fourth dimension: time. For participants in "The Things They Carry Project," the significance of 'The Gleaners' includes the editor's conversation with her daughter, the grief following her daughter's death, and the inspiration to initiate this vital program giving front line health care workers perspective in response to a pandemic. The insight from this conversation, in turn, has helped others, including me. I am perpetually grateful and humbled.

I conceptualize the influence of time by imagining the painting through a kaleidoscope. As the cylinder slowly turns, the original image is fragmented and then projected and reflected off the rhomboid pieces of glass, which are constantly falling into and away from each other. While gentle rotation and shifting of the image continue, a balanced pattern of light and dark, void and substance, is maintained. Over time, conceptualizing this image becomes a reminder that facing a problematic event and finding empathy requires tremendous courage. Describing the outcome as an experience of empathy or its enantiomer, suffering, speaks to our interdependence and the responsibility we have to take care of one another.

PART VI

Healing

INTRODUCTION

Kerry L. Malawista, Ph.D.

HOW DO SOME PEOPLE EMERGE FROM TRAUMATIC, difficult situations stronger than before? Frontline workers in our workshops shared how they found comfort and healing. They practice self-care: exercise, healthful eating and regular sleep. They meditate, make origami, and write. They gather support from family, friends, and community.

Writing allowed our participants the opportunity to step back from their struggle and begin to form a story, a narrative of where they have been and how to move forward. This meant acknowledging the painful times, while also holding tight to any joyful or serene moments. For writing to be healing there needs to be balance of feelings.

In fact, we started our workshops by inviting participants to write about where they find comfort, support, and confidence in their ability to soothe themselves. We structured our groups to assure that the participants were not re-traumatized by writing, and to encourage resilience in frontline workers, we did not dive in with their most painful experiences. We don't want difficult memories to replay as if the person is once again back in the time of stress. Writing needs to be from a point of distance and reflection, a space where the person is not overwhelmed by affect.

Obstetrician Denise Montagnino shares the joy of giving birth. understands the risks and fragility of life and the painful juxtaposition of new life next to so much death.

Despite living in a "400 square foot box" next to a hospital, with sirens blaring, Gavin Morrison, an emergency room nurse, finds small pleasures in sharing a "rinky" twin bed with his partner, the bed covered in his grandmother's tattered quilt, the smell of pasta cooking and a standing vacuum that doubles as a coat rack. It should have been chaos but he finds peace. Gavin doesn't find "too little, it was the whole damn lot."

The impact of the project on the lives of participants was far more powerful than imagined. Many returned to second and third meetings, elated at the solace they found in the process of writing. There are countless examples of great artists and writers using their craft to wrestle with traumatic experiences. Transforming pain into art we gain some mastery over the events.

Paradoxically, while our participants recalled painful experiences and feelings—guilt, anxiety, dread, grief, fear and longing—they also related feeling more enthusiastic at work, with less fatigue, less burnout, and a greater sense of meaning. Processing trauma through writing and reflecting allowed them some control over what happened. Sharing within a group provided the support and validation that they are not alone, and it gave them the opportunity to laugh and cry together. Rather than feeling isolated, writing connected them with others. I have often had the experience of writing a painful memory without any emotion and then, surprisingly, finding myself weeping when I read the piece aloud to another. This experience of having our pain recognized is healing.

Resilience is a constellation of qualities, including the ability to experience optimism, joy gratitude, curiosity, self-control, forgiveness, generosity, and perseverance. A resilient person has a sense of humor, an ability to problem solve, seeks out support when needed and perseveres in the face of hardship and obstacles. Empathizing with others and imagining what they might think and feel (mentalization) are earmarks of resilience, as is the ability to make use of new opportunities and self-reflect. The list could go on, but what underlies all these characteristics is flexibility and the ability to adapt to challenging situations. Yet we cannot forget that for all the resilience an individual may muster, a vulnerability and the sequela of what one has suffered lingers on.

What we can hope for is to maintain the continuity of who we are even while being changed by a harrowing experience and the strength to keep moving forward. Also, the ability to create a coherent self-narrative, that integrates the past, into the present, allowing one to imagine a future. Writing helps in this, offering a way to clarify, re-visit what happened, think about ways the event changed us, and create a new way of seeing the future and discover new truths.

As the poet and writer, Mark Doty, wrote in *Heaven's Coast,* "What is healing, but a shift in perspective?"

The Coat Rack

Gavin Morrison
Emergency Room Nurse ◈ Washington, DC

When I moved here I thought I would finally get away, get some peace and quiet. Little did I know peace and quiet would be traffic honking at all hours of the day and night outside our window. Our space was not much—a 400 square foot box with one big room and one tiny bathroom. We shared a rinky twin bed with his grandma's tattered quilt. The one big room became our kitchen, our dining room, our bedroom, our living room, and our entertaining space. In one corner stood our new "coat hanger." He had thought himself an innovator when he discovered he could hang his red puffer jacket on the back of our standing vacuum and call it a coat rack.

In our tiny, expensive box on Pennsylvania Avenue, we watched as what seemed like an endless line of cars, taxi cabs, and bicyclists marched to and from Georgetown, or any number of possible destinations DC has to offer. The sirens were constant, living next to a hospital. But we would lay side by side on the floor, next to our out-of-commission futon that was busted and beat—it had become a second coat rack. We lay side by side on the floor of our too small box, and we'd gaze into the popcorn ceiling as if it contained the constellations.

And it wasn't much, and yet it was everything. Outside was loud and bright, inside was the smell of pasta baking—his family's recipe, the sound of Anthony Hamilton crooning from his MacBook on the desk, the feel of that stupid old quilt. It should have been chaos, the opposite of a place of peace. Anywhere was peaceful with him. But especially our tiny box full of books, clothes everywhere, and no adequate seating. Especially here was the eye of the storm of the city we found ourselves in. It wasn't too little, it was the whole damn lot.

Healing

Dipanwita Saha, MD, FAAP
Regional Champion for Quality and Safety
PM Pediatrics ● Columbia, Maryland

I had once heard on NPR that wearing many identities helps people be resilient. When one part of you fails, you revel in the other. I have always been proud of my many selves. The partner self, the aunty self, the friend self, the dancer self, the traveler self, and the doctor self.

Being a pediatrician and really maturing into that role over the last decade has been a surprisingly fulfilling identity. Being a pediatrician, you treat the whole family.

Walking new mothers through the first few days of their baby's life, walking a child through their first bone fracture, or even getting them to do something as trivial as burping, has been gratifying.

Over the first few months of the pandemic, I found myself flailing with my doctor identity. Visits over a static video, guiding them to stay at home, left me emptier than I had left expected. The doctor self was carrying a lot more of me than I had realized.

After a few months of mostly telemedicine, it felt great to be in the clinic. Even if it was a shadow of how it had previously felt, even the new way to be a doctor meant wearing and thus creating many layers of barriers: a mask, a face shield, a gown.

He came in that day with his family, hesitantly. The hesitancy quietly shocked me because his lip was gaping open, and I could see the dried blood–

drenched shirt. His father told me that he had wanted to stay home. He wanted his lip to heal on its own, because he was so scared of COVID. For such severe lacerations, I usually refer to the emergency room, but they pleaded.

I went in there with my best nurse, sat down, and reassured him that we were being safe.

I worked with my hands in layers; sweat beads on my forehead, cramp in my back.

On days like this I feel a sense of all-around gratitude and pride: for being there to hold a hand, to heal a child's face, quite literally, to be able to help a family physically and emotionally.

covid pants

Candida Moreira
Relational Trauma Therapist and writer
Vancouver B.C., Canada

my thickest pair of joggers
are
      fleece lined
      and aubergine.
           they offer a reminder
           of softness and comfort
        while zoom-lags intercept my empathy
and the disconnect
grows between us –
(my clients and me).

Zoom therapy is the worst
      and yet i am grateful;
(and lucky that i can still work)
      i will take this chance
      to show up
      imperfectly
      and doing my best.

i will hold hope that
my clients can see themselves
               through my eyes that see
      how they too
              are doing their best;

i hope they know
that my eyes see
(and my heart feels)
the courageous vulnerability
it takes to let themselves be seen
across the immeasurable distance
between us and our screens.

these pants have been
my consistent covid companion.
i used to only wear them
                in winter --
(mainly to feel warm)
        in my chilly basement apartment.

fourteen months ago
    they were the first of five garments
                        granted uniform status
                            by my brain, and
                                (they remain)
        the only item in the bottoms category.

for fourteen months
    i've been rotating four business tops
            while i keep the joggers on repeat:
                        so it is always a party
                                on the bottom.

my clients cannot see the way
            my toes
        stress-curl on their behalf,
        or how my unshaven leg hairs rebel
        in solidarity and rise to the occasion
            of meeting them where they're at:
                frustrated
                        scared
                                ambivalent...
            languishing
            grieving
            sinking
            shedding

and growing
new (metaphorical) limbs:
because everyone needs
at least another set of hands
with which to carry
      all the things
        that covid brings.

my lower limbs have loved being free
      from the leg-prison slacks
                (business casual)
             of pre-covid times;
    gone are the days of too tight
        and too long
           and too much requiring of shoes;
loose, breathable with elastic cuffs
      (and pockets!)
        and space for stretching between sessions:
           barefoot on the backyard grass
              at lunchtime.

four hundred and eighty-three days
          of uniform life and
   my purple joggers
      have grown soft,
     (a little holey)
         threadbare,
           and porous;
         they are no longer
          impervious
     to the light   that wants to get in.

Outside

Dipanwita Saha, MD, FAAP
Regional Champion for Quality and Safety
PM Pediatrics ✸ Columbia, Maryland

In my twenties, I was enchanted by spending time outside, in the woods. It started off as an exploration of myself, that part of me that was distinct from my family, who mostly prefer to spend time indoors, eating and laughing.

Later, it morphed into something that defined my freedom, my health, and my sense of adventure. Today I am walking outside for the first time in weeks, because I am able to do so without coughing and raising alarms to passersby.

There is a path 5 minutes away from my home, and it is part of a nature preserve. I feel more whole today; I am able to feel the cold air on my face. There is a stream that goes through the path. I can hear the water. It is not as loud as in the summer days. I can see some snow on the ground. I see a beautiful redheaded bird zip by me. Later, I learn this is a pileated woodpecker. There is one other person walking, the energetic Korean lady in my neighborhood. Today, she is definitely walking faster than me. I put my mask on fast, we wave at each other. I walk for 5 minutes before I have to pause. I sit down on a chopped wood trunk and look around. I take a deep breath and I feel grounded, I will heal.

Joy

Denise Montagnino, DO, MPH
OB/GYN ● Nashville, Tennessee

I know what they are about to do. I do it every day.

My skin.

My muscle.

My uterus will be severed, separated, ripped, torn, and bleeding. My uterus strong and healthy, kept her safe.

Now it will face the sharp blade.

I felt uneasy, nervous, jittery.

Baby kept moving as though she knew.

She was ready to be ripped, grasped, and grabbed from her watery place.

I know the protocols.

I know the consents.

Sign here.

I know the bright, cold operating room.

Strange it felt to be numb to the slice.

Pressure and tugging.

I knew it would be fast.

Strange it was to fear death in that moment, yet I knew all was safe.

It was as though someone reached deep inside and pulled the life from me.

As she emerged, I felt the release.

The emptiness.

The void.

Then in a blink, the familiar wail. There it was, true and full.
It played again and again in my mind. Oh Joy Begin.
Oh Joy Begin.

Sewing Room

Annie Bustin, RN
Emergency Department at SFGH
San Francisco, CA

In my sewing room, there are photos of family on the walls, a few magical drawings by my daughter of things we both love, and magical trinkets on the shelves. There are bolts of fabric in what I'd like to think are millions of colors from the Universe, several Ott Lites on the sewing table, Alice (my sewing machine), and multicolored spools of thread everywhere—on the table, the carpet, and the ironing board. There are scissors here and there, and a cheap flannel-backed plastic tablecloth on the wall to hold the pieces that I've put together decently—they look ever so beautiful, so calm, so peaceful, and were somehow created with my damaged, tormented, struggling mind.

I can come in here any time of the day, any day of the week, when the traumas from the past start to rear their ugly heads and fuse with the recent ones. And they all have a name, you know, these traumas. They all vie for the top spot of attention from me. Sometimes the hospice patient wins the prize, and sometimes the 16-year-old gunshot-wound victim thinks he should get first place, and then other times it's the lady in the Super Dome, holding her seven-year-old, wondering why we aren't feeding them or giving them water or busing them away from there—and let's not forget the family who can't come in to see their elderly loved one who is dying from COVID.

I go to the sewing room, with photos of family on the walls, and magical trinkets on the shelves, and I use my ability to create something that warms and comforts and silences my damaged, tattooed, and tired mind.

In Person

Janna Sandmeyer
Psychoanalyst ☀ Washington, DC

My body knew before my mind did. Pure joy. I saw her eyes sparkle, and I danced. I didn't know how much I was missing. I had seen her face on the screen, heard her voice on the phone, for months now. The work had been productive. But now, here she was, in the door jamb of her home. She danced back. Our masks could not hide our smiles.

She's an artist and found connection during the pandemic by meeting with friends on her porch, drawing their portraits. When she described the project, I felt the yearning to participate, and the awareness not to intrude. I am not a friend. She offered, "I wanted to invite you, but I didn't know if it would be appropriate, if that would be okay." "I'd love to," I replied. "That would be amazing," she said. And so, we met.

I knew it was as much for me as for her. I knew it was outside the therapeutic frame, but my desire for connection was weighty. I entertained a new frame, a more pliant one.

What I did not anticipate was the embodied joy that engulfed me when I saw her—pure and unencumbered. Other joys during the pandemic were tarnished by losses and nagging anxieties; this one was not.

We sat on the porch, she with pad and pencil. She drew, we talked—in the same manner as during our sessions, meandering and poignant, verbally arm in arm. Her daughter came out on the porch and sat for a spell, regaling me with a story of her cake baking. How delighted I was to meet her in person, this child about whom I had heard so much. I ate a piece of cake. The younger kids made an appearance, clinging to their nanny's legs. The sunset cast a warm hue on the porch, even as the temperature dropped. Two hours passed, she finished the drawing, and it was time for me to go. Her husband came out to meet me, our mutual curiosity giving way to easy conversation. As we said goodbye, she handed me the portrait, with the disclaimer that it didn't look like me. She was right. What I saw in all of the lines was our relationship, etched on a page. I held the portrait close to my chest as I headed for my car.

Little Beach

Joanne Wilkinson, MD, MSc
Medical Director, Family Care Center New England Primary
& Specialty Care ● Pawtucket, RI

My favorite place is the beach at the end of the street near my beach house. We call it Little Beach, and we call the expensive beach club a mile away, with the cabanas, Big Beach. Little Beach is a scruffy, little, seaweed-strewn crescent bound on either side by rocks. It used to be more deluxe, but over the years there has been erosion, and hurricanes, and other things that I haven't paid attention to, but when I am really desperate and need some peace, walking to the end of the street and sitting on one of the flat-topped rocks near the sand always seems to work. The waves come in and go out—not very big, but rhythmic and continuous. The sun sets behind you and the waves become less and less distinct, more and more gray to dark blue. You can see the island across the way, the rich people's summer homes spaced out on the coast, some of them with lights puddling brightly on the water.

I remember one year, my daughter and I walked down to Little Beach on the fourth of July, and instead of fireworks, people were setting off floating lanterns from the rocks. It was magical. We took videos of the incandescent pale blobs rising over the water, meandering in irregular circles, most becoming so small and indistinct that they merged with the stars in the dark sky.

My first love lived on that coast; I can still see his house. He was the person I felt most safe with, over my whole life, and while it makes me sad to look at the A-frame of his family home, pale against the surrounding trees, it also grounds me a little and reminds me that once I trusted someone. I used to come to this beach in college, when I was overwhelmed and needed to cry and figure out my plan for the next portion of my life. I can't say that I ever left the beach with everything figured out, but I left calmer, almost sleepy, as though I had ingested a potion that made me care less about the future.

I have not been to Little Beach since COVID began, even though it is only half a block away from where I have spent several weekends. I've had less time to get away, this year, but another reason, I think, is that I am afraid it won't work for me anymore—that Little Beach will become one of the many things lost this year, and that, having lost it, I will lose all my hope as well. I can't bring myself to sit on the rocks at Little Beach and not feel better, because this is the year that broke me. It feels easier to hold it out there as something that would probably work, if only I could find the time.

Save the Children

Barbara Lovenheim
Writer ● Rochester, NY

The sun has just moved below the horizon.
As she walks in measured footsteps
to the side door, turns the doorknob
it sticks; she presses her shoulder hard
against the wood; it yields.

Joyous sounds of welcome from two young boys
reach her from a distant haze.
She has returned from her work as an ICU nurse
where panic, fear, and death reside with
each COVID patient who is admitted.

She quickly begins to take off her clothes,
shoving them into the washer.
Naked, she runs to the shower to wash
this day's viral residue from her body
before she can kiss and hug her children.

Moving Forward: The Faraway Nearby

Kerry L. Malawista, Ph.D.

IT WASN'T UNTIL THE THINGS THEY CARRY PROJECT launched that I understood I was offering frontline workers a path through pain and trauma, one that I had stumbled upon after the death of my daughter. I had collected the shattered pieces of who I was before her loss, and bit-by-bit, put the shards back together again, creating something new in my life. Writing was the glue.

Trauma disrupts the narrative that we tell others and ourselves of who we are. When that occurs, we are no longer held together securely by our familiar life story. In its place, a revised narrative is required, one that includes a recognition of what came before and at the same time, allows for a vision of a future no longer haunted by the intrusive shock of grief, fatigue, and terror; no longer haunted by all we have seen.

Writing helped me bridge the distance between the faraway of who I was before my loss and the nearby of who I was after. Before my loss, I was a mother of two daughters, and after, I was a mother grieving the unimaginable.

Writing was critical in finding a life of meaning, hope, and renewed joy.

Unexpectedly, the project became one more passageway, one more gift, in my own healing.

My hope was to offer frontline workers a place to bear unbearable feelings, to reflect and reconsider the narrative of their lives—who they were before the pandemic and who they are now, almost two-years later. Sharing alongside others who understand what they have been through lessens the intensity of the intrusive thoughts and feelings of powerlessness they have come to know too well. Where they, too, can collect the shards of the sickness and death they witnessed—all the colors, shapes and textures of the painful memories— alongside the morass of feelings—exhaustion, depression and loneliness—and put them into words.

Gradually some of the anxiety, depression and exhaustion recedes to the background. The pandemic no longer in the foreground of every moment of the day. Then, over time, a new self-narrative can emerge, one that provides continuity with the past, acceptance of the present, and an anchored sense of self to meet the future. Our groups shared more than the pain of Covid, they spoke and wrote about their families, their interests and passions. Group members recognized each other, understanding that they were more than their work during the pandemic.

While these harrowing COVID-19 days may never be completely mastered, the writing workshops inspired a renewed sense of purpose, a greater capacity to envision what might come next, and the possibility of a life restored–of resilience.

These groups offered a microcosm of what we see globally–strangers providing solace to strangers. While the pandemic revealed the many ways COVID-19 separated us–essential workers who didn't have the luxury of self-distancing, from those of us who could work from the safety of home. It brought us together in small and unexpected ways, such as bringing groceries to an elderly neighbor. Participating or watching on television the ritual of thousands of New Yorkers in quarantine taking to their windows, balconies and rooftops to applaud frontline workers. Our 120 workshop leaders wish to express our gratitude for all that they carried for us.

On the fifth of December, twenty-two months into the pandemic, my co-leader, Anne Adelman, and I welcomed six healthcare workers from Rwanda, the Democratic Republic of Congo, Austin, Texas, Birmingham Alabama, Nashville, Tennessee and Atlanta, Georgia into a Zoom workshop. One participant remarked, "I now see so clearly. We are part of a universal tribe. A tribe that transcends all outward differences."

We are global citizens, united by a pandemic. And with that comes civic responsibility: to be vaccinated and for wealthier countries to supply vaccines for developing nations. If everyone doesn't have access to vaccines none of us are safe. Like climate change, we are all in this together.

Responsibility and care for one another is another bridge between the faraway and nearby.

In "Dedications," the final poem in Adrienne Rich's book, *An Atlas of the Difficult World*, Rich imagines the history of the many horrors our country has experienced, inflicted on others, and the unresolved griefs that remain. In her poem she speaks to the "you" that feels exhausted, grief-stricken, answering each hardship with the empathic refrain, "I know you are reading this poem." In the last refrain, Rich writes, "I know you are reading this poem, listening for something, torn between bitterness and hope."

For Rich, the reading of a poem is an act of hope. For The Things They Carry Project participants, writing, saying, "this happened to me" is an act of hope.

Words connect us. Healthcare workers shared their stories, the group listened, and can know that we, the reader, are a witness to the pain, bitterness, and hope.

WORKSHOP LEADERS

Anne Adelman is a clinical psychologist and psychoanalyst with the Washington Baltimore Center for Psychoanalysis and at the Contemporary Freudian Society. She is the co-editor of JAPA Review of Books, as well as co-author and editor of several articles and three books. She is a co-chair of the New Directions Writing Program and maintains a private practice, currently virtually, in Chevy Chase, Maryland.

Devra B. Adelstein is a clinical social worker and child psychoanalyst who practices in Cleveland, Ohio. She works with children, adolescents, adults and families and consults with area schools and clinicians. Ms. Adelstein is on the faculty of the Hanna Perkins Center and the Cleveland Psychoanalytic Center where she teaches child development and psychoanalytic writing and supervises candidates. She is a graduate of the New Directions Writing Program.

Meghan Adler honed her poetry at The Writers Studio in NYC. Her poetry has appeared in Alimentum, *California Quarterly, Gastronomica, The Intima: A Journal of Narrative Medicine, and The North American Review*. Her first book of poetry, *Pomegranate* was recently published with Main Street Rag Press. When not writing or teaching poetry, she teaches literacy strategies to educators and collaborates with neuropsychologists to develop learning plans and implement instruction for students with learning differences.

Sharon Alperovitz, LICSW, Teaching Psychoanalyst, Washington Baltimore Center for Psychoanalysis, Long-Term Writing Group Co-Chair, New Directions in Psychoanalysis, Faculty, Washington School of Psychiatry, Infant and Young Child Observation Program.

Cathy Alter's articles and essays have appeared in the *O, the Oprah Magazine, The Cut, WIRED, Martha Stewart Living,* and *The Washington Post.* She is the author of Virgin Territory: Stories From the Road to Womanhood, the memoir, *Up for Renewal: What Magazines Taught Me About Love, Sex, and Starting Over,* and CRUSH: *Writers Reflect on Love, Longing, and the Lasting Power of Their First Celebrity Crush.*

Sherry Amatenstein, LCSW, is a NYC-based psychotherapist. She has written 3 self-help books, edited the anthology *HOW DOES THAT MAKE YOU FEEL? True Confessions from Both Sides of the Therapy Couch,* and contributed to numerous publications including Vox.com, *New York* and *The Washington Post.* She is a former adjunct writing professor at The New School and NYU and co-led the workshop Women Writing to Change The World at Omega Institute.

Hemda Arad, Ph.D., is a psychoanalyst and supervisor in Seattle, WA, working with individuals and couples. She is a Certified EMDR therapist. Dr. Arad is on the faculty of the Washington Baltimore Center for Psychoanalysis program: New Directions - Writing with a Psychoanalytic Edge. Her book, *Integrating Relational Psychoanalysis and EMDR: Embodied Experience and Clinical Practice* was published in 2018 by Routledge.

Julie Barton is the *New York Times* Bestselling author of *Dog Medicine, How My Dog Saved Me From Myself* (Penguin). She is a graduate of Kenyon College and holds an MFA in Writing from Vermont College of Fine Arts and an MA in Gender Studies from Southern Connecticut State University. Her weekly generative writing class, Unleashed, aims to help people express themselves on the page, judgment free.

Gail B. Bendheim, Psy.D., is a psychologist and psychoanalyst in private practice in New York City. She has a particular professional interest in emerging and young adulthood, and writes occasionally on matters of personal interest

Jessica Anya Blau's newest novel, *Mary Jane,* comes out this spring. She is the author of the bestselling *The Summer of Naked Swim Parties,* and the three other critically acclaimed novels. Her books have been featured on the Today Show, CNN, NPR, and in Vanity Fair, Cosmo, Oprah's Beach Picks, and other national publications.

Deborah Blessing is a clinical social worker and psychoanalyst. She has served on the faculties of the Washington Baltimore Center for Psychoanalysis and Washington School of Psychiatry. Among the positions she has held, Deborah is a former Co-Chair of the New Directions-Writing with a Psychoanalytic Edge program at the WBCP and is the current CoChair of the Observational Studies Program at the WSP. She is in private practice in Washington, DC.

Caroline Bock is the author of *CARRY HER HOME*, winner of the 2018 Fiction Award from the Washington Writers' Publishing House, and the critically young adult novels: *LIE and BEFORE MY EYES* from St. Martin's Press. In 2021, she co-edited *THIS IS WHAT AMERICA LOOKS LIKE: poetry and fiction from DC, Maryland and Virginia* for The Washington Writers Publishing House, which features 100 writers and 111 of their works on the creative state of our Union. Find her often on Twitter @cabockwrites.

Sarah Boxer, a cartoonist, essayist, and critic, is the author of three graphic novels, *In the Floyd Archives, Mother May I?* and *Hamlet: Prince of Pigs.* Her writings have appeared in *The Atlantic, The Wall Street Journal,* and *The New York Review of Books.* For many years she was an editor, arts reporter and photography critic for *The New York Times.* Born in Denver, Boxer lives in Washington, D.C.

Michelle Brafman is a writer and teacher. She is currently on the faculty of New Directions and the Johns Hopkins MA in Writing program where she received the 2019 Excellence in Teaching Award. She is also the author of the novel *Washing the Dead* and *Bertrand Court: Stories* and has been invited to speak to more than 160 audiences about both her work and the creative process.

Mary Brennan is a clinical psychologist who has provided psychotherapy to adults for 40 years. Prior to beginning a private practice in Washington, D.C., she worked in universities including Virginia Commonwealth University (MCV) with medical, nursing and dental students and American University as Director of Psychological Services. Her career has included extensive consultation and therapy on identity, race and gender issues.

Angier Brock, a long-time believer in the healing power of writing and in the value of using writing to help make meaning of one's experiences, has taught for over 35 years in secondary schools and colleges and in small private writing classes. Her poetry and reflective essays often have a spiritual theme. Recent publications include texts set to music by American and British composers and sung by choirs at home and abroad. She lives in eastern Virginia.

Dana Brotman, Ph.D., is a clinical psychologist in private practice in Falls Church, Virginia. She works with children, adolescents and adults and provides clinical supervision. She is also a painter and is currently working on developing her most recent gallery show, *Pillow Book: Pages from a Pandemic*, into book form. In addition, she is writing and illustrating a children's book, *Tiny and Sunflower*.

Kate Brown joined New Directions in 2012. After working in publishing, she earned a Ph.D. from Berkeley and went on to teach at the University of South Carolina, Emory, and SUNY/Buffalo. She has published essays on George Eliot, Christina Rossetti, radical grammar books, and Richard Pryor, among other topics. She currently serves as a writing coach while also writing a novel about Charlotte Bronte, which she is illustrating with needlework.

Abigail Browning, Ph.D., is a researcher, poet, community arts organizer, and literary podcast host. She has poems published in *Yemassee Journal Online, The Greensboro Review, Line Break,* and *RHINO Poetry.* A member of the Carrboro, NC Poets Council, Browning co-organizes the West End Poetry Festival, a free event for all ages. Abigail co-wrote the song "The Dreamer" for Rearrange My Heart, by Che Apalache, Grammy-nominated for "Best Folk Album" (2019).

Tara Campbell is a writer, teacher, Kimbilio Fellow, and fiction editor at Barrelhouse. She received her MFA from American University. She's the author of a novel, *TreeVolution,* and four collections: *Circe's Bicycle, Midnight at the Organporium, and Political AF: A Rage Collection,* and *Cabinet of Wrath: A Doll Collection.* She teaches creative writing at American University, the Writer's Center, Politics and Prose, Barrelhouse, and the National Gallery of Art's Writing Salon.

Dana Cann is the author of the novel *Ghosts of Bergen County* (Tin House). His short stories have been published in *The Sun, The Massachusetts Review, The Gettysburg Review, The Florida Review,* and elsewhere. He's received fellowships from the Maryland State Arts Council, Virginia Center for the Creative Arts, and Mid-Atlantic Arts Foundation, and the Sewanee Writers Conference. He teaches for Johns Hopkins University and The Writer's Center.

Mary Carpenter is a DC-based freelance writer, leading creative writing workshops at The Writer's Center in Bethesda, Md., the DC jail and elsewhere. She has written two middle-grade biographies, including "Rescued by a Cow and a Squeeze" about Temple

Grandin. For more than 30 years, Mary reported on medicine for magazines and websites. She has an M.S. journalism degree from Boston University and an English Literature B.A. from Wellesley College.

Carola Chase is a clinical social worker and child psychoanalyst with a private practice in New York City. She works with children, adolescents, adults, and older adults. She is a member of The Contemporary Society and a graduate of the New Directions Writing Program. She has published two short stories in the *New Directions' Journal*, and several articles in psychoanalytic journals and publications. She is currently completing her second novel.

Tessa Cochran is a psychologist psychoanalyst and graduate of the New Directions Writing Program. She has served on the faculties of SUNY Stony Brook Allied Health Professions and Michigan State's College of Human Medicine. In her clinical practice, she has encouraged

Libby Copeland is an award-winning journalist and author who covers culture and science. She has written for *The Washington Post, The New York Times, The Atlantic and Smithsonian Magazine,* and has authored a book called *The Lost Family: How DNA Testing is Upending Who We Are.* She has served as a media fellow and guest lecturer, and has made numerous appearances as a journalist and cultural commentator on television and radio.

Shelley Costa is the author of *You Cannoli Die Once, Basil Instinct, Practical Sins for Cold Climates, A Killer's Guide to Good Works,* several stories in *The Georgia Review, Alfred Hitchcock Mystery Magazine, Blood on Their Hands, Odd Partner*s, and *The World's Finest Mystery and Crime Stories.* Writing as Stephanie Cole, her most recent books are *Al Dente's Inferno* and *Crime of the Ancient Marinara.*

Kate Daniels is the author of six volumes of poetry, and of the forthcoming prose work, *Slow Fuse of the Possible: On Poetry and Psychoanalysis.* Former poet in residence at Duke Medical Center and Vanderbilt Medical Center, she has taught writing in the New Directions program for fifteen years. She is Professor of English at Vanderbilt University in Nashville.

Steven Demby, Ph.D., is a clinical psychologist and psychoanalyst in private practice in Cobble Hill Brooklyn. He works with adults and older adults. He teaches, supervises, and is on the Board of Directors at the Contemporary Freudian Society. He has published several articles in psychoanalytic and other professional journals. He is a member of the International Psychoanalytical Association.

Lauren Dockett is a writer and book and magazine editor specializing in mental health and social justice. A former caseworker and counselor, she's written for *The Washington Post, Salon,* and NPR. In her current job as senior writer for the National Magazine Award-winning publication, *Psychotherapy Networker,* she writes long-form features at the intersection of mental health and society. Her books are *Facing 30, The Deepest Blue,* and *Sex Talk.*

Molly Donovan began her relationship with New Directions in 1998. A clinical psychologist, she has practiced psychotherapy in Washington, DC, for over 40 years, working with individuals, couples and groups. She currently serves on the faculties of the Washington School of Psychiatry, the Professional Psychology Program at GW University, and the Institute of Contemporary Psychotherapy and Psychoanalysis. She has published professionally and finds journal writing a beneficial exercise.

Micheál Dowling, Ph.D, is a clinical psychologist with a private practice in New York City. He grew up in Ireland. Before college he traveled and worked in a variety of occupations in different countries for over ten years, including factories, computer operations, roofing, carpentry, and nursery school teaching. His areas of interest include immigration, diversity, resilience, and wellness. He has written on the migrant experience.

Martha Dupecher, MSW, Ph.D, is a psychoanalyst and psychotherapist in private practice in Washington, DC. She also trained as a poetry therapist, using poetry to facilitate self-expression and healing in a group setting. Long interested in literature and language, Martha is a reader of fiction, non-fiction and poetry, as well as a writer devoted to memoir and journaling. She is also one of the organizers of the New Directions program.

Karen Earle, LICSW, writer and writing teacher (MFA, 25 years teaching experience). A trauma-informed psychotherapist in private practice, she uses writing as an adjunct to treatment. Her work has appeared in journals, including: *The GW Review, Chaffin Journal, Chaminade, The Denver Quarterly, Hudson Valley Echoes, Metis, Phase and Cycle.* Recent recipient of a MVICW fellowship, she has been involved with New Directions for fifteen years both as graduate and faculty.

Julie Elion is the clinical director of the Center for Athletic Performance and Enhancement and has an MA in counseling. Through her psychotherapy practice she has helped athletes and CEOs achieve their dreams since 2000 as one of the premier mental coaches in sports. Julie focuses on identifying beliefs that block our optimal performance which has helped her gain recognition in multiple articles in *The New York Times, Golf Digest,* and other periodicals as "that lady who helped me to win."

Elissa Ely worked as a community psychiatrist in Boston for 30 years, most of them in street shelters, community clinics and state hospitals. In another life, she was a long-time commentator for "All Things Considered" on NPR, and wrote "The Remembrance Project" a series of radio obituaries about people neither rich nor famous, but highly beloved; ordinary people who lived extraordinary lives.

Cynthia Eyster is a social worker who has worked in individual and group psychotherapy practices. She is a teacher of mindfulness meditation, trained by Tara Brach and Jack Kornfield. She writes poetry and leads meditation and writing workshops in the New York area. She looks forward to participating in The Things They Carry Project.

Cynthia Ezell is a psychotherapist, farmer, ad writer. Her literary work emerges from the intersection of human relatedness and the environment, reflecting an intimate relationship with land and place. Her work has appeared in *The Dead Mule School of Southern Literature, Wordpeace, The Minnow Literary Magazine, Deep Wild Journal,* and *Wineskins.*

Sheila Felberbaum practiced as a Hospice Staff Support Group Facilitator, was a Clinical Nurse Specialist and is a Board Certified Social Worker in private practice on Long Island. A graduate/faculty member of New Directions, her publications and produced plays focus on personal and professional reflections on bereavement, counter-transference and the integration of writing in clinical practice.

Sylvia Flescher is a psychiatrist and psychoanalyst in private practice. She trained in psychiatry at Mount Sinai, where she is on faculty, and is a graduate of the New York Psychoanalytic Institute. She joined the New Directions Writing Program in 1997. Her essay, *Googling for Ghosts: a Meditation on Writer's Block, Mourning and the Holocaust,* was published in *Psychoanalytic Review* in 2012. She is currently at work on a memoir.

Iris Fodor, Ph.D., a Licensed Clinical Psychologist, is Professor Emerita, Department of Applied Psychology, New York University. She has also worked in hospitals. Iris has trained in Cognitive and Gestalt Therapy and is known for teaching and writings about anxiety management, women's mental health and integrative psychotherapy. She has over 40 publications and has mentored student and academic writers. Recent work focuses on experiential writing and life story. website: dririsfodor.com

Elizabeth Bales Frank is a novelist and essayist whose work has appeared in *The New York Times, Glamour, The Sun, Lit Hub, Barrelhouse*, and other publications. Her novel *Censorettes* was released in 2020. She earned a BFA from NYU's Tisch School of the Arts and an MLIS from the Pratt Institute. She lives in Astoria, NY.

Diana Friedman is an award-winning writer whose work has appeared in numerous publications including *New Letters, The Huffington Post, Newsweek,* and *The Baltimore Sun.* Teaching is also integral to Diana's commitment to the writing community: she has taught writing at Writopia Lab, the University of Maryland, facilitated small group workshops, and currently co-leads a creative collective of artists, and a long-term writing group at the New Directions Program at the Washington Baltimore Center for Psychoanalysis.

Stephanie Friedman holds an MFA in Writing from Vermont College of Fine Arts, and has taught for many years in the Writer's Studio, a creative writing program for adult students at the University of Chicago. Her fiction, essays, and poetry has appeared in venues such as *Michigan Quarterly Review, theminnesotareview, RiverTeeth*'s "Beautiful Things" series, and was listed among the "Notables" for the year in *Best American Short Stories.*

Ilana Giannini is a television writer turned psychotherapist who works with trauma survivors, individually and in groups. She established Voices of Warriors, a trauma group therapy program at Wright Institute Los Angeles and consults with Women in Film, establishing groups for women subject to predators in the workplace. Ilana believes creative work, coupled with a supportive group process, are powerful antidotes to the isolation and shame attendant to trauma.

Martha Blechar Gibbons is a nurse psychotherapist, nurse practitioner, qualitative researcher, educator, and author. She maintains a private practice in Washington D. C. where she provides clinical supervision as well as psychotherapy and psychopharmacology for children, adolescents and adults, offering a diversity of treatment modalities.

Andrea Greenman, Ph.D., is supervisor and faculty member at NYU PostDoc and Training Analyst at the Contemporary Freudian Society. Having served as President of CFS for the past three years, she is interested in the problem of how organizations can fail their members, and how that can be repaired. She is an alumna of New Directions, and in private practice (remotely) on the Upper West Side of New York.

John Gualtieri did his doctoral studies at University of Buffalo, State University of New York receiving his Ph. D. in 1983. He began learning about the treatment of post-traumatic stress disorder during his pre- doctorate internship at the V. A. Medical Center in Buffalo.

Caroline Hall, Ph.D, is a therapist in private practice in Asheville, North Carolina where she sees individuals and couples. She worked for years with pregnant and postpartum women as a therapist in the Women's Mental Health Program at Georgetown Outpatient Psychiatry where additionally she trained psychiatric residents and medical students on the topic. She has published on psychological responses to childbirth.

Paula J. Hamm, LPC, Psychoanalyst, Teaching Narrative Clinical Writing at the Washington Baltimore Center for Psychoanalysis, Graduate of New Directions Writing Program, Chair of Ongoing Discussion Group on the Psychodynamics of Religion/Spirituality at the American Psychoanalytic Association.

Melanie S. Hatter is an award-winning author of two novels and one short story collection. Selected by Edwidge Danticat, Malawi's Sisters won the inaugural Kimbilio National Fiction Prize, published by Four Way Books in 2019. *The Color of My Soul* won the 2011 Washington Writers' Publishing House Fiction Prize, and *Let No One Weep for Me, Stories of Love and Loss* was released in 2015. Melanie received a master's in writing from Johns Hopkins University.

Nancy Heneson is a medical writer, poet, essayist, teacher, and editor. She had led workshops at The Writer's Center in Bethesda, Maryland and the New Directions Writing Program of the Washington-Baltimore Center for Psychoanalysis. After 30 years interpreting science for a wide variety of audiences, she now edits research papers and helps authors develop books. Her essays and poems have appeared in medical journals and on Stoop Stories and public radio.

Sandra Hershberg, MD, an adult and child psychiatrist and psychoanalyst. Supervising and Training Analyst at the Washington Baltimore Psychoanalytic Institute and The Institute of Contemporary Psychotherapy and Psychoanalysis and on the Editorial Boards of Psychoanalytic Inquiry and Psychoanalysis, Self and Context. Published papers focus on the female gaze in art and psychoanalysis, the relationship between biography and psychoanalysis, mother/daughter relationships, and maternal responses to childhood disability.

Alison Hicks is the author of two poetry collections, a poetry chapbook, a novella, and an anthology. Her forthcoming collection is winner of the 2021 Birdy Prize from Meadowlark Books. Her work has been named a finalist for the Beullah Rose Prize from *Smartish Pace,* and has appeared in *Eclipse, Gargoyle, Permafrost,* and *Poet Lore,* among other journals. She is founder of Greater Philadelphia Wordshop Studio, which offers community-based writing workshops.

Sybil Houlding, MSW, graduate of the Western New England Institute for Psychoanalysis, where she is Faculty Dean. Private practice in New Haven, treating individuals, couples, and families. Teaching interests include unrepresented states, and trauma. 2009 graduate of New Directions, published journal articles, book chapters, and book reviews. Editorial Board member of JAPA.

Eileen Ivey, MSW, is a psychotherapist and poet in Chevy Chase, MD, a lover of metaphor, and author of a chapbook, *Out of Order.* Her poems have been published in *Ekphrastic Review, Calyx, District Lines, Beltway Poetry Quarterly, NewVerseNews* and elsewhere. In addition to practicing psychotherapy, Eileen has served on the faculty at GWU School of Medicine, helping medical students discover their patients' stories and explore their human reactions as physicians.

Rachel Jadkowski, Ph.D, is a Clinical Psychologist practicing in the Green Mountains of Vermont. Currently she sees clients over zoom, as well as outdoors while hiking, skiing, and snowshoeing. Rachel is attuned to her clients' relationships not only with themselves and other people, but with the more-than-human world of the Wild. She enjoys working with other writers and exploring all clients' creativity as an essential part of being human.

Susan Jaffe, M.D., Psychiatrist, Psychoanalyst; Residency Training Supervisor, New York University School of Medicine and Mount Sinai School of Medicine; Graduate and Faculty, the New York Psychoanalytic Institute; Member, New Directions Writing Program; Private Practice, Midtown Manhattan; Working on first novel.

Susan Kane, LCSW, is a psychotherapist in private practice in New York City treating adults, couples and adolescents for over thirty years. She specializes in working with people with eating disorders and has presented her original theory on the "Impact of Neglect in the Transference/Countertransference Paradigm nationally. She is a graduate of New York University School of Social Work, the Women's Therapy Centre and the New Directions Writing Program.

Liat Katz is a licensed clinical social worker and a writer. Her personal essays have appeared in the *Washington Post, NY Times, Washingtonian, Lilith, Bethesda Magazine, Kveller.com, Kevin MD.com, Contemporary Psychoanalysis, and Pulsevoices. org*. She has created and taught a therapeutic writing group at an abused women's shelter. She writes with humor and through the lens of a mother, a patient, a clinician, and someone just muddling through life.

Colleen Kinder has written essays and articles for *The New York Times Magazine, The New Republic, VQR, The Wall Street Journal,* the *Atlantic.com, Creative Nonfiction,* and *Best American Travel Writing 2013*. A graduate of the Iowa Nonfiction Writing Program, she has received fellowships from Yaddo, MacDowell, Ucross and the Fulbright. She is the co-founder of the magazine *Off Assignment,* the editor of *Letter to a Stranger* (forthcoming, Oct 2021), and teaches for Yale Summer Session in France.

Rachel King is a graduate of the New Directions program and is currently a degree candidate in the Masters in Writing Fiction program at Johns Hopkins. She has spent her career in biotechnology and is CEO of GlycoMimetics, a company she co-founded. She earned her B.A. from Dartmouth College and her MBA from Harvard Business School.

Natalie X. Korytnyk, Ph.D., is a clinical psychologist in private practice in downtown Washington, DC providing individual and couples psychotherapy. Formerly an Assistant Professor of Psychiatry and Behavioral Sciences Professor at George Washington University Medical School, she has also been the Chief Psychologist of Inpatient Psychiatry at Walter Reed Army Medical Center and on staff at the National Rehabilitation Hospital. She is an alumna of the WBPC New Directions Writing Program.

Delia Kostner, Ph.D., is a psychologist and psychoanalyst practicing in New Hampshire. She is on the faculty of the Boston Psychoanalytic Institute. She is the guiding teacher of Souhegan Insight Meditation and has written and lectured on the interface of psychotherapy and Buddhism. She is also an avid outdoors person and backpacker.

Jessica Leader is the author of Nice and Mean (Simon & Schuster), a middle-grade novel about seventh-grade girls. A long-time English teacher, she has coached students to write award-winning pieces for contests such as GLSEN's No Name-Calling Week, Actors Theatre of Louisville, and DC's One World Foundation. She earned her BA from Brown University and her MFA in Writing for Children and Young Adults from Vermont College of Fine Arts.

Annette Leavy, LCSW, is a psychoanalyst, writer and teacher. She is the former editor of the journal, *Psychoanalysis and Psychotherapy*. A graduate of the New Directions program, she is a member of the Philadelphia Wordshop Studio. Her lyric essay, "COVID Dreaming" will appear in the spring issue of *Caveat Lector*. Her story, "The Walnut Queen," will be published in the forthcoming issue of *The Capra Review*.

Leslie Leitner is a psychotherapist in LA. She holds a certificate in psychoanalytic psychotherapy from the Los Angeles Institute and Society for Psychoanalytic Studies. Her clinical interests include working with adults and families dealing with anxiety, depression, complex trauma, grief, illness and death. Leslie splits her time between private practice and the PCH Treatment Center where she works with families and has led therapeutic writing groups for several years.

Jeanne Lemkau practices clinical psychology in Chapel Hill, North Carolina. She is Professor Emerita of Boonshoft School of Medicine of Wright State University where she taught behavioral science for 25 years. She earned her MFA in creative nonfiction in her fifties and enjoys writing and coaching the writing of others. She has authored numerous academic publications as well as a memoir, *Lost and Found in Cuba: A Tale of Midlife Rebellion.*

Joanie Liebermann, M.D. - A former internist involved in the early days of the AIDS epidemic, I am currently a psychiatrist and psychoanalyst in private practice in Washington, DC and on the faculty of the GWUMC Obstetrics and Gynecology Department. I have been an instructor in the New Directions Psychoanalytic Writing Program for over 15 years and am a writer of poems and essays.

Ona Lindquist, LCSW, is a psychoanalyst in private practice in Brooklyn, NY. Her published and presented works include: *What a Blackbird Told Me is Real and Alive - the relationship between poetry and the use of language in psychoanalysis;* Swimming in Space *- fragments of a therapy in verse;* A Barter to Be *- a psychoanalysis in art and verse;* One Glorious Noise *- how the voice of Bruce Springsteen entered my consulting room.*

Tarpley Long is a Teaching Analyst at the Washington Baltimore Center for Psychoanalysis. She is the Editor of *Psychbytes,* a monthly publication of short essays on psychoanalytic thinking in everyday life. She has been a small group leader in the New Directions program of the Washington Baltimore Center for Psychoanalysis. Her Letters to the Editor have been published in *The Washington Post* and *The New Yorker* magazine.

Barbara Lovenheim, Ph.D., taught for 17 years in the English Department at Monroe Community College where she created the courses Literature of the Holocaust and Witchcraft. She has taught in the Master of Arts in Liberal Studies at Dartmouth College and Nazareth College. She has an MFA in Creative Writing poetry, publishing in *miller's pond, Hazmat, Scapegoat Review* and *A Handful of Dust,* plus two books of poetry.

Marion Maclean is a retired teacher of high school literature and writing. In 1981, she trained to become a teacher of writing and writing consultant through the Northern Va. Writing Project. She has led many workshops around the country, published a book about classroom research co-written with another teacher, and has overseen production of in-house publications. She attended New Directions from 2005-2008, returning regularly as participant or faculty since 2014.

Kerry L. Malawista, Ph.D., is a writer and psychoanalyst and co-chair of *The New Directions in Writing* program. Her essays have appeared in *The New York Times, The Boston Globe, The Baltimore Sun, The Washington Post, Zone 3, Washingtonian Magazine, The Huffington Post, Bethesda Magazine, Arlington Magazine, The Account Magazine,* and *Delmarva Review,* which nominated her for a Pushcart Prize. She is co-author of four psychology books with Columbia University Press. Her first novel, *Meet the Moon,* was released in 2022 with Regal House Publishing.

Tammi Markowitz-Inscho is a reformed lawyer turned freelance writer. She is currently working on her first novel and teaching creative writing workshops. Her personal essays have been published in the *Philadelphia Inquirer* and the online magazine *Manifest-Station*. Tammi is an Amherst Writers and Artists certified creative writing workshop leader.

Molly McCloskey is the author of 5 books—a memoir and 4 works of fiction—and is currently collaborating on a book about early intervention in treating schizophrenia. She has taught workshops at various universities in the US and Ireland, and has been a teacher at New Directions for 3 years.

Elizabeth McKamy, MSW, was trained and worked with individuals and groups at the Professionals in Crisis Program at the Menninger Clinic in Topeka, Kansas and led multiple Physicians in Transition groups at the Menninger Center for Applied Behavioral Science. Since retirement from private psychotherapy practice, and particularly during the Covid pandemic, she provides consultation to senior colleagues as they navigate complex practice and personal challenges that impact their own retirement considerations.

Aimee Molloy is the author of two novels, *Goodnight Beautiful* and *The Perfect Mother*, which was a *New York Times* bestseller and translated into more than twenty-five languages. She has also written several non-fiction books and for publications such as *The New York Times, The Washington Post,* and *The Guardian.*

Marc Nemiroff, Ph.D., is a clinical psychologist who has worked with a variety of groups in clinical, professional, religious, cross-cultural and community settings. He is the author of a text on working in groups, as well as a memoir of his decade of work with disenfranchised children and families in the Mumbai slums. He also served as a consultant to Global Roots, a non-profit providing assistance to impoverished children and families in Asia and Africa.

Ruth Neubauer, LCSW, is a teacher, a writer, and a long-time psychotherapist. She graduated New Directions in 2003, remains on the faculty of the Washington School of Psychiatry, and teaches lifelong learning at OLLI-DU in Denver, Colorado where she currently lives. She also maintains a private practice, and facilitates groups for Women Over 65 using impromptu writing as a tool to explore relevant issues. Ruth looks forward to being part of the Things They Carry Project.

Jenifer Nields, M.D., is an Assistant Clinical Professor of Psychiatry at the Yale School of Medicine where she supervises residents in the long-term psychotherapy program. She teaches psychoanalytic psychotherapy at WNEPS and has published on the neuropsychiatric effects of Lyme Disease, psychotherapy with medically ill patients and psychoanalysis and religion. Early in the COVID-19 pandemic, she volunteered as part of the 1:1 counseling program for Yale-affiliated frontline healthcare workers.

Liisa Ogburn has written for *The New York Times, Runner's World, Academic Medicine*, and others, previously taught physicians and residents how to tell patient stories in a program she founded at Duke University. She currently writes on aging for WRAL and runs an elder consultancy, as well as speaks widely. She and her son published *Looking for Heroes: One Boy, One Year, 100 Letters* in 2016.

Gay Carol Parnell is a Psychologist Psychoanalyst in Private Practice in San Diego, Ca since 1977. She was certified by the American Psychoanalytic Association in 2003. She graduated from New Directions in 2003. She has been teaching courses in Psychology since 1974, graduate courses since 1980. She has been a clinical supervisor since 1980. Dr. Parnell has given presentations and training in Switzerland, Italy, Mexico and the Netherlands since 1977.

Ann Pearlman, a writer, artist and former therapist living in Ann Arbor, MI. , is the author of two nonfiction books, *Keep the Home Fires Burning* and *Inside the Crips*, two memoirs, *Infidelity* which was made into a film and *Eyes on a Sparrow*. Her novels, *The Christmas Cookie Club, A Gift for My Sister,* and *The Lottery* were international best sellers.

Nancy Peltzman is a Chicago psychoanalyst who graduated from the New Directions in Writing Project. She has taught small groups of therapists at the Chicago Center for Psychoanalysis for the past 13 years. Over the last two decades she has worked with many highly traumatized individuals, and repeatedly seen the healing properties of self-expression.

Sarah Perry's memoir, *After the Eclipse*, was a New York Times Book Review Editors' Choice; other work has appeared in *Off Assignment, The Guardian,* and elsewhere. Perry is a 2020-2022 Tulsa Artist Fellow and has received fellowships from the Edward F. Albee Foundation, VCCA, Playa, and The Studios of Key West. She has taught at Columbia University, Davidson College, Manhattanville College, and numerous community writing centers.

Judith Pitlick, MA, LPCC, is a child, adolescent, and adult psychoanalyst and psychotherapist in private practice, Shaker Heights, Ohio, who works with individuals, couples, parents, families, and supervises psychoanalysis and psychotherapy. A graduate in psychoanalysis from the Hanna Perkins Center and the Cleveland Psychoanalytic Center, she is on the faculty of both programs. She a recipient of the Edith Sabshin Teaching Award of APsaA, and a Clinical Instructor, CWRU School of Medicine.

Billie Pivnick, Ph.D., is a psychoanalytic psychologist in private practice in NYC, specializing in treating individuals and families suffering from traumatic loss. She is faculty/supervisor in the William Alanson White Institute Child/Adolescent Psychotherapy Program and the New Directions Writing Program. Co-creator/co-host of the *Couched* podcast, she also won APA's 2015 Schillinger Award for her essay "Spaces to Stand In: Applying Clinical Psychoanalysis to the Relational Design of the National September 11 Memorial Museum".

Christie Platt, Ph.D., is a clinical psychologist. In addition to seeing clients in private practice, she provides pro bono psychotherapy to veterans and psychological evaluations for asylum seekers. She is a practitioner of mindfulness meditation and is interested in contemplative care for those with serious illnesses and persons facing death. She has published a number of essays. She is looking forward the opportunity to support this writing project.

Judith Ruskay Rabinor, Ph.D., is a licensed clinical psychologist in private practice in New York City and a consultant to the Renfrew Center Foundation. Judy teaches writing classes, coaches writers, has published dozens of articles and three books, most recently: *The Girl in the Red Boots: Making Peace with My Mother* (2021).

Elizabeth Rees is the author of *Every Root a Branch* and three award-winning chapbooks. Her poems have appeared in *Agni, The Southern Review, Partisan Review, Carolina Quarterly,* and *Kenyon Review,* among many other journals. She has taught at many universities, as well as at The Writer's Center in Bethesda, MD. In addition to teaching privately, she has also worked as a poet-in-the-schools for the Maryland State Arts Council since 1994.

David Rowell is the author of the novel *The Train of Small Mercies* (2011) and *Wherever the Sound Takes You: Heroics and Heartbreaking in Music Making* (2019), an exploration of the inner lives of musicians. He has taught literary journalism in the MFA department at American University and is the deputy editor of *The Washington Post Magazine.*

Helen Betya Rubinstein's essays have appeared in venues like *Literary Hub*, *Jewish Currents*, *The Kenyon Review*, and *The New York Times*. She holds MFA degrees in fiction and nonfiction, from Brooklyn College and the University of Iowa, respectively, and her work has been honored with fellowships from the MacDowell Colony, Yaddo, and many others. She teaches at The New School and works one-on-one with other writers as a coach.

Laura Scalzo's fiction has appeared in journals and online literary magazines, including *Hobart, Ellipsis Zine, Reflex Fiction, Grace in Darkness, Grace & Gravity*, and as a finalist in the 18th Annual Writer's Digest Short Short Story Competition Collection. Her YA novel, *The Speed of Light in Air, Water* (One One Two Press, 2018) was a five-star, #1 Amazon Bestseller in Literary Fiction.

Cathy Schen, M.D., an adult and adolescent psychiatrist and psychotherapist, teaches psychiatry residents at Harvard Medical School. She has published papers in academic journals on race in supervision, walking psychotherapy, writing about patients, and other topics. She farms at a nearby organic farm and has published essays in literary journals on farming and doctoring, landscape and memory, and Willa Cather. She is currently writing about her father.

Linda B. Sherby is a psychologist-psychoanalyst in practice in Boca Raton, Florida. She is the author of the book *Love and Loss in Life and in Treatment* written from the perspective of both a widow and a psychotherapist. The book interweaves memoir with her work with patients.

Jayme Shorin, LICSW, maintains a private practice of psychotherapy in Cambridge MA. Jayme had been the Associate Clinical director of the Victims of Violence Program at the Cambridge Health Alliance at Harvard Medical School for 32 years She graduated from Smith SSW in 1988, and trained in sensorimotor psychotherapy and Internal Family Systems therapy.

Susan Shreve is the author of 15 novels, a memoir, 5 anthologies and 30 books for children. She founded the MFA in Creative Writing program at George Mason University and taught at Columbia School of the Arts, Princeton University, and Goucher College. She's received a Guggenheim Award and a National Endowment grant for fiction, the Jenny Moore Chair in Creative Writing, and the Grub Street

Prize for non-fiction. She is the co-founder and former chairman of the PEN/Faulkner Foundation.

Emily Simmons received an MFA in Creative Writing poetry from Sarah Lawrence College. She taught creative writing to at-risk youth, then created a riding program specializing in neurodivergent students. She lives with her spouse, two children, four horses and alpacas, three dogs and cats, along with a ridiculous number of chickens.

Julia Slavin is the author of *The Woman Who Cut Off Her Leg at the Maidstone Club and Other Stories* and the novel, CARNIVORE DIET. She is the winner of the Rona Jaffe Foundation Writers' Award, GQ's Frederick Exley prize, and a Pushcart Prize.

Aria Beth Sloss is the author of *Autobiography of Us,* a novel. Her writing has appeared in Glimmer Train, the Harvard Review, Ploughshares, Joyland, One Story, Martha Stewart Living, and *Best American Short Stories 2015*. A graduate of the Iowa Writers' Workshop, she is the recipient of fellowships from the Iowa Arts Foundation, Yaddo, and the Vermont Studio Center. She lives in New York City with her family.

Janna Malamud Smith is a writer, a psychotherapist, and an experienced writing workshop leader. She has lectured and published widely nationally and internationally. She is the author of four books, including *An Absorbing Errand: How Artists and Craftsmen Make their way to Mastery (2013)*. She has recently finished a book about fishing and fishermen on an island off the coast of Maine.

Madelon Sprengnether is Regents Professor Emerita of the University of Minnesota, where she taught literature and creative writing. Her recent books include: *Great River Road: A Memoir* (New Rivers Press, 2015), *Near Solstice: Prose Poems* (Holy Cow! Press, 2015), and *Mourning Freud (*Bloomsbury Academic, 2018).

Sally Steenland is a writer and consultant. She worked at the Center for American Progress, a national think tank, and before that was an op-ed columnist for The Philadelphia Inquirer. She has written two best-selling books, *The Magnetic Poetry Book of Poetry* and the award-winning *Kids' Magnetic Book of Poetry*. Her short stories have appeared in literary journals and been anthologized. She received a BA from Calvin College and an M.Ed. from Howard University.

Jonathan Stillerman is a clinical psychologist and Certified Group Psychotherapist with a private practice in Washington, DC. As faculty at the Washington School of Psychiatry, he teaches in three training programs, supervises students and serves as Dean of the National Group Psychotherapy Institute. Alongside his clinical work, Jonathan is a published poet, and in a former life, he co-founded Men Can Stop Rape, non-profit empowering male youth to prevent gender-based violence

Judith Stone is the author of the nonfiction books When She Was White and Light Elements. Her work has appeared in *The New York Times Magazine, O, Smithsonian*, and many other publications. She was on the founding board of The Moth, and is a storytelling instructor in its community outreach program.

Jennifer Swift is a writer who loves to teach students of any age or background, those who are eager as well as those who are wary. Her work is published in *The Sun Magazine*, and she is currently working on a novel based on her aunt's experience growing up in Australia during World War II. She has a Ph.D. in English and an MA in Writing.

Sara Mansfield Taber is a writer, social worker, and developmental psychologist. She is author of the award-winning *Born Under an Assumed Name: The Memoir of a Cold War Spy's Daughter*, the writer's guide *Chance Particulars: A Writer's Field Notebook*, books of narrative journalism, and essays published by *The Washington Post* and *The American Scholar*. She offers individual therapy and literary coaching, and leads writing workshops for memoirists and health professionals.

Liza Nash Taylor was a 2018 Hawthornden International Fellow and received an MFA from Vermont College of Fine Arts the same year. She was the 2016 winner of the San Miguel Writer's Conference Fiction Prize. Her work has appeared in *Microchondria II*, an anthology by the Harvard Bookstore; *Gargoyle Magazine*; *Deep South*; and others. A native Virginian, she lives in Keswick, in an old farmhouse which serves as a setting for her novels.

Elizabeth Thomas, MTS, MSW, Ph.D., is a psychotherapist, specializing in relationships and with a background in spirituality. In the past, she has written and presented clinical papers; currently, her writing is focused on memoir and fiction. Elizabeth has been both a student and a member of the faculty of New Directions since 2009. She is active in several writing groups. She lives in the Blue Ridge Mountains of Virginia.

Deirdre Timmons' 30-year career has spanned newspaper reporting, magazine writing, Internet editing, screenwriting, and directing documentaries. In 2020, she published her debut memoir, "Brain Candy," about being treated for a fast-growing, inoperable, malignant Medullo Blastoma. In 2021, she released an award-winning documentary, "Land of the Sweets: The Burlesque Nutcracker." Deirdre graduated Smith College, where she studied English Literature and theoretical math. She lives in Seattle.

Valerie Tripp is the award-winning author of American Girl books about Felicity, Josefina, Samantha, Kit, Molly, and Maryellen as well as the Welliewisher and Hopscotch Hill School series. Currently, Tripp is writing a STEM series for *National Geographic Kids*. She has adapted classics for Sterling Publishers, and has written numerous leveled readers, songs, stories, skills book pages, poems, and plays for educational publishers.

Anna Vodicka's essays have appeared in *AFAR, Brevity, Guernica, Harvard Review, McSweeney's Internet Tendency, Ms., Paste,* and *Best Women's Travel Writing*. She is a grant recipient of Artist Trust and 4Culture, and has earned residency fellowships to Vermont Studio Center and Hedgebrook. Anna teaches creative writing at Seattle's Hugo House and to women incarcerated at the King County Jail.

Kate Wechsler, LCSW, is New York City psychotherapist in private practice since 1990 treating adults, couples and adolescents. Consulting in several preschools in Brooklyn NY, she specializes in offering Parent Guidance services especially to families with young children. She is a graduate of New York University School of Social Work, Postgraduate Center for Psychoanalytic Training and the New Directions Writing Program.

Anne Wild-Rocheleau, Ph.D., practices in West Stockbridge, MA. She trained at the Austen Riggs Center, Duke University and Dartmouth. She graduated from the Berkshire Psychoanalytic Institute where she is now faculty. She is part of the New Directions community and will be co-directing the program, Sex Talk: On the Couch and On the Page. Her practice includes adults, teens, children and families, and she enjoys writing memoir and fiction.

Anne Wotring, Ph.D., is a retired writing teacher and researcher at George Mason University and Fairfax County high schools. Her expertise is in cultivating writing as a potent transformational tool for psycho-spiritual and intellectual growth and development. Her M.A. is in English Education and Ph.D. in Human and Organizational Studies. As a Life Coach for the past 20 years, she specialized in helping individuals navigate life transitions.

Jennifer Bort Yacovissi's debut novel, *Up the Hill to Home*, tells the story of four generations of a family in Washington, D.C. from the Civil War to the Great Depression. Her short fiction has appeared in *Gargoyle* and *Pen-in-Hand*. Jenny reviews regularly for the Washington Independent Review of Books, and serves on its Board of Directors. She has served as chair/program director of the Washington Writers Conference since 2017.

Martha Addy Young is the recipient of two Individual Artist Grants from the Washington D.C. Commission on the Arts and Humanities and a Poet Fellowship from the Martha's Vineyard Institute of Creative Writing. Runner-up for the *Bellevue Literary Review's* poetry prize, and a finalist for the Larry Neal Writer's Award and the Crosswinds Poetry Award. Her poem "Dusk in Dupont Circle" was featured in *Poetry Daily*. She holds an MFA and is trained in the AWA writing method.

Laura Zam is a certified trauma professional and author of *The Pleasure Plan*, a memoir about reclaiming her body after sexual violation. Laura's essays/articles appear in *The New York Times*, *Salon*, *HuffPost*, and other publications. For the past 20 years, Laura has conducted healing-through-writing workshops. She's worked with U.S. military, teens from conflict regions, and assault survivors. Laura has an M.F.A. in Creative Writing from Brown University.